SHORE BETS!
THE DELMARVA FUN GUIDE

Also by Jim Duffy/Secrets of the Eastern Shore:

• *Eastern Shore Road Trips #1*
27 One-Day Adventures on Delmarva

• *Tubman Travels*
32 Underground Railroad Journeys on Delmarva

• *Eastern Shore Road Trips #2*
26 MORE One-Day Adventures on Delmarva

• *You Wouldn't Believe*
44 Strange and Wondrous Delmarva Tales

Website
SecretsoftheEasternShore.com

Facebook
Facebook.com/SecretsoftheEasternShore

Bookstores, retail shops, and other purchase options
SecretsoftheEasternShore.com/product-category/books

Feedback
SecretsoftheEasternShore@gmail.com
443.477.4490

SHORE BETS!
THE DELMARVA FUN GUIDE

A Secrets of the Eastern Shore Book
By Jim Duffy

— · · ● · · —

Published by Secrets of the Eastern Shore
Cambridge, Maryland
ISBN: 978-1-7356741-7-9

Cover Design: Jill Jasuta
Interior Design: Paul Clipper
Research, Writing, and Other Help:
        Paul Clipper & Makena Duffy

Feedback
SecretsoftheEasternShore@gmail.com
443.477.4490

More Stories
SecretsoftheEasternShore.com

INTRODUCTION

————— ··•·· —————

Another weekend approaches. Weather looks good. You're feeling the itch to let loose, have fun, break out of the routine. Hit the road for a day, maybe the weekend.

What to do?

Ah, there's the rub. The whole Delmarva Peninsula is within striking distance, from down on Virginia's Eastern Shore and up through the Maryland shore and over to Delaware. How do you narrow things down from the hundreds of possibilities—towns and parks and museums and more? Which have fun events? Which have cool discoveries nearby?

The answers are hard to find, actually. We're talking 14 counties in three states, each with its own tourism website and online calendar. How many hours can you blow on planning? Is that why you keep going back to the same old familiar places?

Wouldn't it be nice if somebody gathered up all the fun events and the best destinations into an easy-to-use book? That book is in your hands. Don't mention it.

Shore Bets! isn't a writerly affair, full of stories and clever turns of phrase. It's more of an idea factory. That slew of fun events. The bevy of cool destinations. Flip through: It's your all-in-one guide to Delmarva discoveries.

A few things you'll learn:

• Where to see the world championship of muskrat skinning (page 155).

• How to get chased down a beach by two people in a cheesy bull costume (page 62).

• Which little museum has a Cheeto that you really need to see (page 183).

• How to enlist in a zombie army hellbent on invading a small town (page 124).

It's not all wackiness. *Shore Bets!* will help you find oysters, crabs, beer, peaches, tall ships, scrapple, and more. It will inspire you to discover new towns, to find fresh natural wonders, and to join in celebrations of our watermen, our farmers, our artists, and our history.

Another weekend approaches ... and here's hoping this book helps you make the most of it.

Jim Duffy

FIVE EASY PIECES: HOW THE BOOK WORKS

— • •●• • —

My goal is to make it super easy for you to find fun events and destinations. I've been tracking those things for Secrets of the Eastern Shore for nearly a decade. I am sorry to report that you will have to do a little work. But it's easy work.

(1) Links stink.
I am not including hundreds of web-address links in these pages, complete with httpses, forward slashes, and hyphens. That's because they go dead sometimes, and they get outdated. You'd curse me out whenever that happened. We don't want that.

(2) Search engines are great.
Type the name of an event or destination into a search bar. No forward slashes involved.
• If it's an event, maybe include the current year. You might even include the state abbreviation, too, lest you end up by accident at the Centreville Day festivities in Ohio.
• The vast majority of the time, you'll be all set, straight away. On occasion, you might have to hunt around for a minute, but you'll get there.

(3) Month of Fundays!
That is the Secrets of the Eastern Shore newsletter. It comes out around the first of every month. If I do my job right, that newslet-

ter will contain current working links to details for the events in this book.

Find Secrets of the Eastern Shore on the web. Sign up. Or send me an email and I'll load you up manually: SecretsoftheEasternShore@gmail.com. No spam. No selling of addresses.

Bonus: Each issue will have more events than the ones listed in this book.

(4) Fair warnings.

There are a few places in this book where I say something like, "This event is going to sell out early." In those cases, don't wait for the newsletter. You might miss out.

There are approximately 9,537 beer festivals on Delmarva these days. I picked a few and included them. The same goes for small-town festivals. I did the best I could. Thanks for your patience with that.

(5) What's nearby?

When traveling to an event or destination, I usually make two or three other stops in the neighborhood. The Destinations section of this book is one great place to get ideas.

Plus, at the end of listings here, you'll find the name of local tourism offices. Pop that into your search bar to find nearby fun stuff. Make sure you're in the right state. There are counties elsewhere with the same names as some of our counties.

One other thing: Happy wandering!

Map of the Regions

Near the top of events and destinations in the pages that follow is a line identifying which region of the Delmarva Peninsula we're talking about. Here is a map of those regions.

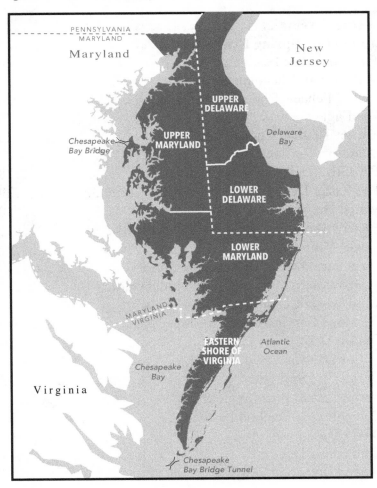

TABLE OF CONTENTS

Shore Bets!

PART ONE: EVENTS

CHAPTER ONE: SPRING EVENTS

Two Chocolate Festivals

Rehoboth Chocolate Festival
Early March in Rehoboth Beach, Del.
Region: Lower Delaware

St. Michaels Chocolate Festival
Early March in St. Michaels, Md.
Region: Upper Eastern Shore of Maryland

Winter always seems to linger too long, doesn't it? At these two events, you'll be able to fill that on-the-eve-of-spring void with sweet indulgences while making jaunts to towns renowned for their abundance of visitor-friendly diversions.

The older of the pair is in Rehoboth Beach, where the festivities date to the town's centennial in 1990. Almost always a sellout, the one-day event usually happens indoors in a conference center, so you'll be sheltered from the late winter elements if necessary and yet within a stone's throw of the beach, the boardwalk, and the downtown if Mother Nature cooperates. Sample chocolate creations by local restaurants, professional bakers, and amateurs alike. A celebrity chef or two will likely be on hand, signing books and doing demos.

The younger St. Michaels event dates to 2019. A good number of restaurants serve up chocolate-inspired specials over two days while hotels and B&Bs offer festival packages that might include extravagances on the order of "chocolate" spa treatments. The most popular event is a Saturday Chocolate Crawl, which involves wandering the downtown from tasting station to tasting station, gobbling up sweet samples while sipping on local wines, beers, and spirits.

Tourism info:

• Rehoboth Beach: Visit Rehoboth and/or Southern Delaware Tourism

• St. Michaels: St. Michaels Business Association and/or Talbot County (Md.) Tourism

THE EAGLE FESTIVAL

Mid-March in Cambridge, Md.
Region: Lower Eastern Shore of Maryland

Celebrate our national bird at the 30,000-plus-acre Blackwater National Wildlife Refuge, where nesting pairs of eagles abound. While there, you'll get to see why the marshlands of Delmarva rank as a natural wonder of the first order, blessed with breathtaking scenery and abundant wildlife.

Many experts say Blackwater is home to the largest population of nesting pairs on the East Coast outside of Florida. During the Eagle Festival you'll be able to sign on for educational programs and guided tours or choose to explore on your own by grabbing a map of eagle "hot spots." Other bird species will get some time in the limelight as well—educational sessions in recent years have been devoted to falcons, owls, hawks, and other raptors. Kids will have plenty to do. Recent highlights on that front include making wooden bird boxes and testing archery skills.

TIP JAR: On your way to or from Blackwater, take a short detour to Old Trinity Church in Church Creek, Md. That gorgeous house of worship dates to the late 1600s and still houses an active congregation. Its beautiful waterfront graveyard is the resting place of several Revolutionary War heroes as well as Anna Ella

Carroll, a local woman who famously served as friend and advisor to Abraham Lincoln.

Tourism info: Dorchester County (Md.) Tourism

HARRIET TUBMAN ANNIVERSARY WEEKEND

Early/Middle March in Cambridge, Md.
Region: Lower Eastern Shore of Maryland

Underground Railroad conductor Harriet Tubman was born into slavery in the countryside outside of Cambridge, Md. This gorgeous landscape is where she endured the agonies of bondage and set out in search of freedom. Here, too, is where she developed the courage, smarts, and skills that would allow her to return time and again to help others escape slavery.

Her life is celebrated pretty much every day in Dorchester County, where murals and statues and markers abound, all attesting to her status as an American hero of the first order. Located tenish miles below Cambridge, the first-rate Harriet Tubman Underground Railroad Visitor Center is a joint operation of the National Park Service and the Maryland Department of Natural Resources.

In early spring, the center—it's more of a museum, actually—schedules various special presentations and activities on a weekend that falls close to the anniversary of Tubman's death on March 10, 1913. In recent years that has meant author talks, storytelling sessions, musical performances, and historical re-enactors.

TIP JAR: If you want to embark on a larger journey in Tubman's footsteps, my book, *Tubman Travels: 32 Underground*

Railroad Adventures on Delmarva, will help lead the way. Or find your way online to the Harriet Tubman Byway—that's a great option, too.

Tourism info: Dorchester County (Md.) Tourism

DELMARVA HERITAGE DAY

Late March in Pocomoke City, Md.
Region: Lower Eastern Shore of Maryland

Some of the region's top decoy carvers set up shop during this weekend in the Delmarva Discovery Museum, which is dedicated to telling the stories of life on Delmarva through the centuries. Consider it an opportunity to take a deep dive into the artistry, traditions, and subculture of decoy making.

Carving didn't start out as an art form. Up until the early 1900s, the wood ducks carvers created were everyday tools in the hunting trade. Wherever you found ducks and hunters, you'd find a few carvers, churning out wooden birds to make some bucks on the side. Things changed when factories started making cheaper, mass-produced decoys. After that, only the best of the best carvers made the transition into a modern-day world where decoys often end up in museums and private art collections.

This event is about showcasing that artistry. You'll meet and chat with veteran carvers as they work on pieces while set up in the middle of the exhibit rooms. Be sure to spend time with the museum's first-rate exhibits. Step outside and you'll be in downtown Pocomoke City. Cross the street and stroll the historic Pocomoke River in Cypress Park.

Tourism info: Worcester County (Md.) Tourism

THE GREAT DELAWARE KITE FESTIVAL

Good Friday (sometimes late March, sometimes April) in Lewes, Del.
Region: Lower Delaware

This high-flying, kid-friendly festival full of Easter activities is a great way to soar into spring. It's got a fun back story, too. According to local legend, a visiting dignitary from India, the Maharajah of Bharatpur, challenged the governor of Delaware to a kite-flying duel in 1969. Scheduling complications caused the governor to call in his second, Lt. Gov. Eugene D. Bookhammer. In an upset for the ages, the underdog politician either won that duel or came oh-so-close.

I've combed through old newspapers from those years, and I have my doubts about the legend. But this much is for sure: Bookhammer did take part in kite duels out on Cape Henlopen. One was against a guy from the suburbs of Baltimore who claimed to be the kite-flying champion of the world. Neither Bookhammer nor the people of Lewes seemed to care whether that guy's specious claim was true.

Eager for springtime fun, they turned the match into an annual gag. Spectators came. Newspapers reported breathlessly on bits of pro-wrestling-like braggadocio between the lieutenant governor and his opponent. One year, the public address announcer accused Bookhammer of trying to blind the opposition by way of ... super-bright plaid pants.

Everyone had a lot of laughs, and somehow, this gag turned into the oldest kite festival in the country. Held on Good Friday at Cape Henlopen State Park, the Great Delaware Kite

Festival mixes in a bevy of Easter festivities with various kite-flying contests and aerobatic displays. A big Easter egg hunt for children 12 and under kicks things off. A personal appearance by a certain bunny adds to the Easter atmosphere. The kite competitions unfold in categories broken down by age of contestants and kite types. Awards go to the most unusual homemade kite and the most attractive one, among other categories. Some brave souls enter the Kite Ballet, flying in time to prerecorded music.

Tourism info: Lewes Chamber of Commerce and/or Southern Delaware Tourism

THE EASTER DECOY AND ARTS FESTIVAL

Easter Weekend (sometimes late March, sometimes April) in Chincoteague, Va.
Region: Eastern Shore of Virginia

The Easter timing here is fitting. The Easter Decoy & Art Festival is the first big show of each new year for the East Coast decoy-carving community, so there is a feeling of renewal in the air as everyone convenes, usually at the Chincoteague Combined School. Carvers come from as far away as Maine and Florida in addition to states closer to home.

For most of the event's history, decoys were the sole focus of attention, but organizers have spread their wings in recent years, inviting other artists to join in. You'll be able to meet and greet photographers, painters, and other creative souls while making the rounds. A good number of carvers will likely be toiling away on new pieces while chatting with visitors. Who knows, maybe you'll find a little something to take home?

In addition to artists, vendor displays also focus on home and hunting paraphernalia—garden décor, birdhouses, wildlife feeders, hand-carved model boats, duck calls, and the like. Soups and desserts will be available—if that's not enough, the restaurants along Main Street or on bustling Maddox Boulevard will be short rides away. Lots of awards get handed out as the show draws to a close. In a cute touch, children under 12 get to vote for a favorite artist by placing a ribbon at his or her display table.

TIP JAR: If you're a fan of unique holiday décor, check the schedule for the silent auction of wooden Easter eggs. Many are hand carved or hand painted by artists at the event.

Tourism info: Chincoteague Chamber of Commerce and/ or Eastern Shore of Virginia Tourism

MOUNT HERMON PLOW DAYS

Early April in Salisbury, Md.
Region: Lower Eastern Shore of Maryland

Get in touch with the original meaning of horsepower at this event on a working farm in the countryside east of Salisbury. Wear shoes that can get handle a little muck, as you won't want to miss the opportunity to get behind a plow and a couple of work-horses for a hands-on taste of real old-fashioned farm work.

A family-friendly affair, Mount Hermon Plow Days was started up by a popular local Baptist preacher, Oren Perdue, to pay tribute to the farming heritage of Delmarva and give modern-day kids and kids-at-heart a memorable experience of the way things used to be. Think petting zoo, pony rides, wheelbarrow races, and hay-bale-rolling contests.

You will probably have opportunities here to get your

picture taken in an old stagecoach, go for a hay-wagon ride, and observe a horse-powered corn-shelling operation. Artisans will be hard at work in tents on such old-school tasks as canning, blacksmithing, and yarn spinning. Re-enactors will be bringing to life scenes from farming days gone by. Lots of antique farm equipment will be on display. The live music will most likely be country-flavored gospel.

Tourism info: Wicomico County (Md.) Tourism

EASTERN SHORE SEA GLASS AND COASTAL ARTS FESTIVAL

Early April in St. Michaels, Md.
Region: Upper Eastern Shore of Maryland

The shards of glass that star in shows like this enter the sea as worthless litter. Only after 20, 30, or 40 years of being submerged do they re-emerge with the look of nature-made jewels, edges all smooth and frosted to perfection after so much exposure to salt and all that grinding up against rocks and shells. It's no wonder that this glass sparks a sense of joy in so many people.

Most of the artists you'll meet at this festival held on the grounds of the Chesapeake Bay Maritime Museum spend countless hours beach-combing along remote stretches of sand in search of their raw materials. This two-day show is your chance to see what they make with that glorious old garbage. In recent years, the festival has featured 75 or so artists displaying work that runs from jewelry to home décor to abstract art. Food, drink, and live music will be on the schedule. So, too, will educational sessions and artist presentations. In a bonus, your ticket gives you free run through a museum complex that covers 18 acres and includes multiple exhibit buildings and more than 100 historic vessels.

Tourism info: Talbot County (Md.) Tourism

LEWES TULIP FESTIVAL

Early/Middle April in Lewes, Del.
Region: Lower Delaware

This springtime classic on Delmarva will have you wandering a sweet beach town while it celebrates its Dutch roots through displays of 20,000-plus tulips. The first Europeans to settle in Lewes were Dutchmen who arrived in the exceedingly early year of 1631. Planning to find their fortunes by catching whales and running a trading post, they dubbed the place Zwaanendael, or Swan Valley, before getting wiped out by Indians. More Dutchmen followed in their wake, ruling the roost here until a fleet of British warships showed up in 1664.

This festival is one of several ways during the year that the modern-day people of Lewes pay homage to those Dutch roots. Spread out over two spring weekends, the event is built around those 20,000-plus tulip bulbs planted all over town. You can find your way to the blooms in self-guided fashion by picking up an event map. In recent years, there have been special exhibits, flower-arranging demos, and tulip sales on the agenda as well.

The festival began in 2009, but the story behind it goes back to 2002 when a fledgling little group of community volunteers decided to roll up their proverbial sleeves and use flower power to beautify their town. Today, Lewes in Bloom has more than 200 members. Their work has helped the town become a four-time winner in the national America in Bloom competition.

Tourism info: Lewes Chamber of Commerce and/or Southern Delaware Tourism

OPEN FARM DAY AT BROWNSVILLE PRESERVE

Mid-April in Nassawadox, Va.
Region: Eastern Shore of Virginia

The appeal of Open Farm Day is equal parts nature, history, and family fun. For a span of 326 years, these 1,250 acres on Virginia's lower Eastern Shore were in the hands of one family, the Upshurs. From a colonial-era wharf on Brownsville Creek, they shipped corn up the Atlantic to markets as far away as New York and New England. The oldest section of their Brownsville House dates to the days when Thomas Jefferson was president.

Today, the Nature Conservancy manages the land as a preserve to support resident and migrating birds, as well as other wildlife. Every day throughout the year visitors can access a three-mile hiking trail through part of the preserve, but access to the rest of Brownsville is a no-go ... except during this event.

The old Upshur home will probably be open for tours. Join in on naturalist-led strolls, take boat rides on Upshur Creek, and enjoy old-school wagon rides. The forests, farm fields, and marshlands along those tours are chock full of deer, foxes, raccoons, herons, and eagles. Educational sessions, old-fashioned games, picnic lunches, and live music will likely be on the bill, too.

Tourism info: Northampton County Chamber of Commerce and/or Eastern Shore of Virginia Tourism

EASTERN SHORE OF VIRGINIA HOUSE AND GARDEN TOUR

Middle/Late April in locations that vary from year to year
Region: Eastern Shore of Virginia

Virginia Garden Week is a hugely popular affair that lasts eight days and offers thirtysome excursions all over Old Dominion—from up in the mountains to down in the big cities. Year in and year out, however, the tour of the Eastern Shore ranks among the most popular offerings.

No wonder: This stretch of Delmarva is a treasure trove of glorious houses from centuries gone by. Consider Eyre Hall, which is always included as a headline attraction on this tour. Located near Cheriton, the estate is still in the hands of a family that arrived in 1623. The home dates to 1760. The gardens, which were laid out when Thomas Jefferson was president, might rank as the oldest continuously cultivated formal gardens in the country. The boxwoods and crepe myrtles are as ancient as things get when it comes to those European-style gardens on this side of the Pond.

Other tour destinations vary from year to year, but they are usually clustered around a central, interesting locale. Properties near Onancock were the focus in one recent year. Another year, the tour was set in and around Cape Charles. No worries: There will be lots more interesting places to choose from in the years ahead.

Tourism info: Eastern Shore of Virginia Tourism

WARD WORLD CHAMPIONSHIP WILDFOWL CARVING COMPETITION

Late April in Ocean City, Md.
Region: Lower Eastern Shore of Maryland

The incredible biological detail carved into the wooden birds on display here will have you shaking your head in disbelief as you wander from one display to the next. The show usually involves more than 1,000 artworks. Some $60,000 in prize money gets doled out during World Championship weekend, with the range of competitors running from gifted schoolchildren up through the ranks of previous world champs. Some of the biggest names in the field will take time out to lead classes and share tricks of the trade.

Now more than 50 years old, this long-weekend extravaganza usually features a big awards ceremony and an auction of "world-class" works on Saturday afternoon. A Friday dinner honors "Living Legends" of the field. Vendor tables display a wider range of nature-themed art, while the Kids Corner offers the younger set a chance to tackle craft projects. Find your way to the "Old Bird" display if you are curious to see collectibles that were carved prior to 1950.

The event's traditional location is the Convention Center in Ocean City. There have been occasions in recent years where some or all of the affair was held at the Ward Museum in Salisbury.

Tourism info: Ocean City (Md.) Tourism and/or The Ward Museum

OXFORD DAY

Late April in Oxford, Md.
Region: Upper Eastern Shore of Maryland

Set on a bend in the Tred Avon River, postcard-pretty Oxford is one of the oldest towns on Maryland's Eastern Shore, tracing its history to the 1660s. For many of the colonial years that followed, it served as an official Port of Entry for foreign goods, drawing commercial ships from all over the world.

It's a quiet place today, home to around 700 people. While enjoying this celebration of spring, you'll probably wonder at some point if perhaps every last one of those residents is volunteering to help out with logistics. Festivities happen all over town—in parks, churchyards, hotels, even aboard boats—so you'll have ample opportunity to savor the strolling pleasures of the lovely old homes on Morris Street and the waterfront "Strand" with its thin stretch of beach. If you get tired, hail a volunteer-powered pedicab.

The main event is a civic parade down Morris Street. A fun Battle of the Bands pits local high school units against each other. Both a car show and a dog show will probably be in the mix. The music stage is set up in Town Park, perched on a bluff that serves up a glorious view of the Tred Avon. Both the Oxford-Bellevue Ferry and the skipjack *Nathan of Dorchester* should be offering rides, if the unpredictable spring weather cooperates.

TIP JAR: Oxford boasts a pair of interesting museums that you should visit—the Oxford Museum, focused on the broad scope of local history, and the Water's Edge Museum, featuring the stories and accomplishments of the region's African Americans.

Tourism info: Talbot County (Md.) Tourism

Milford Bug and Bud Festival

Late April/Early May in Milford, Del.
Region: Upper Delaware

A great excuse to wander an old shipbuilding town, the Bug and Bud party has been known to draw thousands of visitors to enjoy its mix of a parade, live music, vendor shopping, and more. The back story here is pretty darn cute. In the 1970s, the local second-graders in Miss Molly Brown Rust's classroom at LuLu Ross Elementary School petitioned the state legislature to declare the six-legged *Coccinellidae* the official insect of Delaware. The success of that endeavor is the reason so many people in Milford (and their dogs) don ladybug costumes for the morning parade that kicks things off at Bug and Bud.

If past years are a guide, stages and vendors will be lined up on the main drag of Walnut Street as well as along the winding Mispillion Riverwalk. Expect to find fun surprises along the way—paddle-boat rides, pizza-eating contests, and chalk-art competitions have been in the mix in recent years.

Tourism info (Milford straddles the border between two counties):
Kent County (Del.) Tourism
Southern Delaware Tourism (Sussex County).

OCEAN CITY SPRINGFEST

Early May in Ocean City, Md.
Region: Lower Eastern Shore of Maryland

Once upon a time, Memorial Day marked the start of the beach tourism season. That is just what the powers that be in Ocean City set out to change more than 30 years ago by launching this four-day festival on the first weekend of May. Shopping is one big draw, as scores of arts and crafts vendors show off goods under gigantic white tents. Music is another: Evening concerts featuring big-name country and pop acts are ticketed affairs, while daytime performances by more than a dozen regional acts are free.

A third draw is probably the biggest attraction of all, however—and that is simply the warm spring sunshine landing on the sandy beaches of Ocean City. Folks flock to Springfest by the tens of thousands to bid a not-so-fond farewell to the colder months. The event happens just below the boardwalk, so it will be an easy matter to stroll up in search of nostalgic and sinful indulgences. Fries? Check. Taffy? Check. Funnel cake? Check.

You'll be able to play the arcade games, ride the Ferris wheel—pretty much everything will be back open and rolling. Don't forget to kick off your shoes and get some of that warm sand between your toes. Go ahead, dip those toes in the ocean while you're at it. The calendar may not say so in an official sense, but summertime has arrived.

TIP JAR: The event that follows here is on the same weekend and quite nearby.

Tourism info: Ocean City (Md.) Tourism and Worcester County Tourism

BERLIN JAZZ & BLUES WINE & BREWS

Early May in Berlin, Md.
Region: Lower Eastern Shore of Maryland

Traditionally held on the Saturday of the big Springfest weekend in nearby Ocean City, this music-and-libations block party involves two or three stages running live music all afternoon and into the evening. Those stages are set amid a pretty, historic downtown that might look familiar, as it was the backdrop for the romantic comedy antics of Julia Roberts and Richard Gere in "Runaway Bride."

As the title implies, lots of regional brews and vintages will be available for your sipping pleasure. A Wine Tasting option is available as a ticketed affair. Local restaurants will be serving up street food, while regional artists show off their work in vendor tents. Needless to say, the shops and museums will be open—and busy!—as well.

Tourism info: Berlin Chamber of Commerce and/or Worcester County (Md.) Tourism

CHINCOTEAGUE SEAFOOD FESTIVAL

Early May in Chincoteague, Va.
Region: Eastern Shore of Virginia

Time to test your gluttonous limits at this all-you-can-eat affair. The event dates to the 1960s, but the island's reputation as a seafood mecca dates back a lot further. In the 1800s, "Chincoteague Oysters" were regarded as a delicacy as far away as Philadelphia and New York City. The so-called "Oyster King of New York," Thomas Downing, was born a free black man near Chincoteague in the late 1700s. In more modern decades, countless island restaurants have earned measures of fame for their oyster, clam, and seafood creations.

Expect a big crowd at Tom's Cove Park—the event is traditionally held on the first Saturday of May. The seafood will be fresh and local, prepared by a mix of restaurants, "festival chefs," and civic groups. In recent years, the menu has featured littleneck clams, raw oysters and clams, clam fritters and strips, single-fried oysters, fried fish, steamed shrimp, clam chowder, grilled chicken, sweet potato fries, boardwalk fries, hush puppies, and cornbread. There will be a salad bar, too, if you care. Local bands will be playing. Artisans will be showing off works.

TIP JAR: The seafood festival sells out pretty early most every year, so snag your tickets well in advance. Table seating is limited, so maybe bring folding chairs and a blanket or little table.

Tourism info: Chincoteague Chamber of Commerce and/or Eastern Shore of Virginia Tourism

DOVER DAYS FESTIVAL

Early May in Dover, Del.
Region: Upper Delaware

Immerse yourself in colonial times at this celebration of First State heritage held on the Dover Green in the state capitol complex. In its modern incarnation—the event dates back to the 1930s—the focus is on a big Saturday bash that starts off with a morning parade and then shifts into a slate of old-school, family-friendly fun that runs from maypole dancing and a colonial artisans village to historical re-enactors and vintage automobiles.

Upwards of 200 vendors have been known to set up shop. While in the neighborhood, be sure to stop at the several small museums and houses that make up the First State Heritage Park—they are all within strolling distance. The Delaware State Archives usually offer a special Dover Days tour that includes rare public access to storage areas that are otherwise hermetically sealed to preserve the most priceless of Delaware documents, including the one by which the "First State" ratified the U.S. Constitution and earned its nickname.

TIP JAR: In recent years, the Downtown Dover Partnership has gotten into the act as well, creating an evening afterparty downtown. Called H3 for "History, Heritage, and Hops," it showcases the work of Delaware's craft breweries. Live music, food trucks, and more.

Tourism info: Kent County (Del.) Tourism

KENT ISLAND DAY

Early May in Stevensville, Md.
Region: Upper Eastern Shore

If you're the sort of traveler who zooms across Kent Island in a big rush on your way to the beach resorts on one side or the big cities on the other, Kent Island Day is your chance to slow down and get to know a place full of interesting stories. For starters: This was the site of the first-ever European settlement in Maryland, a fort built in 1631.

Traditionally held on the third Saturday in May, Kent

Island Day happens in pretty downtown Stevensville, a two-block run of shops, eateries, and old architecture tucked away near the westernmost exit on the Eastern Shore side of the bridge. The day begins with a classic small-town parade, then settles into an afternoon street festival with food vendors, craft displays, kids' activities, and music. Several small-town historic attractions will be open for tours—an old post office, an old train station, an old bank, and a couple of historic homes. In recent years, the event has featured blacksmiths at work, exotic animals, exhibits of archaeological artifacts, and old-school military encampments.

Located several miles away in Chester, the Kirwan House features an old general store filled with fascinating throwback merchandise, much of it straight from the collection of the family that used to own the place. It will probably be open for tours on Kent Island Day, thanks to the Kent Island Heritage Society.

Tourism info: Queen Anne's County (Md.) Tourism

GALENA DOGWOOD FESTIVAL

Mid-May in Galena, Md.
Region: Upper Eastern Shore of Maryland

This celebration of spring usually kicks off with a big morning parade with floats and marching bands making their way along a route famous for a run of dogwood trees planted in the 1950s. The festival that follows is at the local firehouse, where you will find vendors, kids' games, cornhole boards, crafts demonstrations, a car show, a flea market, and more. Local music, too.

Like just about every other small town on Delmarva, Galena is full of interesting back stories. When the town was first settled in the 1760s, it was called Downs' Cross Roads after a tavern of that name. George Washington dined here on his way to the First Continental Congress. He must have enjoyed it, because he stopped again on the way back.

The name Galena came along when the town was officially incorporated in the 1850s, and this is where things take a turn toward mystery. In several old history tomes citing vague and untraceable sources, there is talk of a mining operation here in the early 1800s that extracted silver from a kind of lead sulfide scientists know as galena. Supposedly, the owners of that mine shut it down to prevent the enemy from finding it during the War of 1812. As far as I can tell, no expert has found real evidence to back up this tale.

An alternate explanation of the name touches on that same galena-as-silver business. By these accounts, Galena is a reference to the "sterling character" of the local populace, something you will be able to judge for yourself while mixing and mingling at the Dogwood Festival.

Tourism info: Kent County (Md.) Tourism

HORSESHOE CRAB & SHOREBIRD FESTIVAL

Late May in Milton, Del.
Region: Lower Delaware

Discover a natural wonder of the first order at this two-site festival celebrating that lovable ancient oddball, the horseshoe crab. Every spring on the shores of Delaware Bay, those prehistoric-looking "crabs"—actually, they're more closely related to sea spiders—clamber up on the beaches in droves as part of an annual migration ritual in which females dig holes in the sand to lay eggs—lots and lots and lots of eggs. A single lady horseshoe can lay up to 120,000 eggs during this yearly mating window.

These creatures don't just look prehistoric. They've been waddling up onto earth like this for 220 million years, since before the dinosaurs appeared. The eggs of those lady horseshoes are packed with nutritional goodness, which is why a gazillion ravenous shorebirds stop here for a few days during their spring migration. Those birds gobble up those eggs like peanuts, trying to rebuild strength and pack on body weight before continuing on the long journey ahead.

The Horseshoe Crab & Shorebird Festival is a two-site affair held in recent years on the Saturday of Memorial Day weekend. Your starting point is downtown Milton, Del., where there will be live music, educational booths, vendors, food trucks, and kids' activities. Shuttle buses take folks from Milton out to Prime Hook National Wildlife Refuge for bird walks, crafty activities, and more.

TIP JAR: You can craft your own horseshoe adventure by visiting the run of beaches above Lewes during the high tides that roll in with new and full moons during May or early June. The DuPont Nature Center near Slaughter Beach is a great place to get oriented while doing that.

Tourism info: Southern Delaware Tourism

RIDGELY STRAWBERRY FESTIVAL
Late May in Ridgely, Md.
Region: Upper Eastern Shore

Commune with the Caroline County locals at this sweet, small-town celebration of a fruit that once reigned supreme on the

Delmarva Peninsula. That era coincided with the arrival of the railroad in the 1800s, giving local farmers a reliable and high-speed way to get their fruit up to big-city markets while still fresh. Scores of railroad cars packed with ice would roll every day into towns like Ridgely, with the line of berry wagons from local farms waiting to unload sometimes stretching for miles.

The boom times ended in the early 1900s, but they are still celebrated every spring on Delmarva—and the town of Ridgely puts on what's probably the biggest of those events. Set in shady Sutton Memorial Park, the event kicks off with an interdenominational church service in advance of a noontime parade through town. The biggest attraction at the park in the afternoon is strawberry shortcake prepared by volunteers with the local Lions Club. Be prepared to wait in a long line to get in on that action. Vendors aplenty, food trucks, and live music as well.

Tourism info: Caroline County (Md.) Tourism

A Day in Old New Castle

Late May in New Castle, Del.
Region: Upper Delaware

During the nation's oldest continuous house-and-garden tour, you'll stroll cobblestone streets past music stages, vendor tables, historical "encampments," kids' games, and more in a Delaware River town that started life as a fort built to protect passing commercial traffic and military vessels. The Dutch flag flew here during part of the 1600s, followed by a Swedish one, and then a British one. This is where William Penn landed in 1682 to take control of a Pennsylvania colony that then included all of Delaware.

45

New Castle has been about the work of celebrating all that history for a long time now—the house and garden tour at the heart of this event dates back to the 1920s. The dozen or so stops on that tour nowadays will take you into a mix of private homes, public buildings, and little museums. Along the cobblestone way, you'll likely pass musicians, pirates, a beer garden, colonial craftspeople, food vendors, and military re-enactors. One replica tall ship or another will probably be docked down at the town's pretty waterfront park. Carriage rides have been offered in recent years, too.

Tourism info: New Castle County (Del.) Tourism

NATIONAL REVOLUTIONARY WAR RE-ENACTMENT AND COLONIAL FESTIVAL

Late May in Earleville, Md.
Region: Upper Eastern Shore of Maryland

The heady days that gave birth to our country come to life during this annual two-day festival at an old plantation set on a sweet little peninsula just off of the Sassafras River. With more than 600 re-enactors portraying a mix of loyalist (bad guy) and continental (good guy) troops, it's one of the country's largest Revolutionary encampments.

You'll be able to visit camps and learn up close about the rigors of soldiering life. You'll watch units do drills, show off tactics, and even engage in skirmishes and battles. The grounds at Mount Harmon will be filled with other bits of living history as well. If past attractions reappear, that array will include cooking at the hearth and scrapple making. Food and beverage vendors, plus a colonial marketplace where you'll be able to visit with artisans while browsing their goods.

The setting is as impressive as the event. The story behind the 200-acre Mount Harmon Plantation dates to 1651, when Lord Baltimore himself awarded the land to a man named Godfrey Harmon. By the time of the Revolution, Mount Harmon had become a thriving tobacco plantation. The manor house, which should be open for tours, dates to the late 1700s. Several sweet strolling trails meander off from that house, serving up a succession of impressive waterfront and rural vistas.

Tourism info: Cecil County (Md.) Tourism

ART AND MUSIC ON THE FARM

Late May in Machipongo, Va.
Region: Eastern Shore of Virginia

You can put this event on your hit list for obvious reasons—it's a big fun party, it's in the great outdoors, and it's traditionally held on the Memorial Day holiday weekend. Located just off of the Route 13 highway, the Barrier Islands Center makes its home at the gorgeous Almshouse Farm, a National Register of Historic Places property that did duty for a century and a half as a "poorhouse" where down-on-their-luck locals lived and worked.

But you can also single this one out for more specialized reasons. If you love old-school roots music—think bluegrass, gospel, ragtime, blues, Appalachian fiddle, and more—this event showcases Virginia's top talent. And if you love meeting artists, there will be three dozen or so talented souls set up in tented exhibits showcasing paintings, photography, pottery, and more.

The artistry of local chefs, vineyards, and breweries will be represented, too.

TIP JAR: If you or a loved one dabble in musicianship, scour the schedule for the workshops that some performers put on during the day, sharing insights into the traditions and techniques that go into their toe-tapping artistry.

Tourism info: Northampton County Chamber of Commerce and/or Eastern Shore of Virginia Tourism

BOWERS BEACH BUCCANEER BASH

Late May in Bowers Beach, Del.
Region: Upper Delaware

Here is your pirate-flavored Memorial Day weekend excuse to get off the beaten path and discover the throwback charms of a little fishing town perched where the Delaware Bay meets the magnificently named Murderkill River. Bowers Beach is a tad too small and far afield for the throngs of visitors who descend on the resort towns of Lewes and Rehoboth Beach during warm-weather weekends, but that out-of-the-way business is central to the charm of the place, as it has helped Bowers stay truer than other towns to its roots as an old fishing village.

The Buccaneer Bash is the town's biggest party of the year. Real-life pirates did, in fact, prowl the coastline of the First State, and the historical timing of that is central to the event's motto: "Party like it's 1699!" The Bash will have pirate re-enactors roaming through town, showing off their sword fighting, musketry, and cannon-firing chops. Craftspeople demonstrate more utilitarian endeavors, such as blacksmithing, glass blowing, and woodworking. In recent years the Buccaneer Bash has also served up a mix of workshops (knot-tying, for example) and presentations (weaponry, female pirates). The First Delaware Militia might be on hand to fight the pirates. Plus, pirate-flavored music and a pirate bar brawl that breaks out in a local tavern and soon spills out into the street, becoming a peg-legged, eye-patched mini-riot.

Tourism info: Kent County (Del.) Tourism

CHESTERTOWN COLONIAL TEA PARTY

Late May in Chestertown, Md.
Region: Upper Eastern Shore of Maryland

Things take a Revolutionary turn in this three-day festival held in a town that for quite a few stretches of the 1700s ranked as Maryland's second-largest city, behind Annapolis. Today, it ranks second to Annapolis in a different category—the number of still-standing buildings that date to before the American Revolution.

Those Revolutionary days are the focus of this Memorial Day weekend festival, which draws throngs of visitors into Chestertown for performances and events that run from down on the Chester River waterfront up several long blocks into the heart of downtown and over to pretty Wilmer Park.

Many of Chestertown's museums and historic sites will have talks, performances, and other events. Food vendors, libations, and crafts displays will pop up at every turn. In a "colonial village," you'll be able to tour a military camp and meet the likes of seamstresses and blacksmiths. Street performers will be doing their thing—dancers, singers, storytellers, more. Other highlights

49

in recent years: period marching bands, old-school puppet shows, and a "colonial conjurer."

The event is based on a bit of oral history about how some Chestertown patriots boarded a British ship and tossed a bunch of tea overboard in May of 1774 to show support for compatriots up in Boston. Whether it's true or not—well, probably not. But the legend still serves as a fine excuse for thinking about what heady times the mid-1770s must have been in towns like this. My favorite part of the Tea Party festivities is the street theater—a staged reenactment of this legend that unfolds right along High Street, complete with musket fire.

Tourism info: Kent County (Md.) Tourism

CHAPTER TWO:
SUMMER EVENTS

St. Michaels Brewfest

Early June in St. Michaels, Md.
Region: Upper Eastern Shore of Maryland

The wandering itch that takes hold as the warm weather starts to rise should be in full force by the time this one-day bash pops up on your calendar. Usually held on the Saturday after Memorial Day (which means rare occasions when it falls on the last day or two of May), it's geared toward beer aficionados eager to sample interesting firkins, rare brews, and seasonal concoctions—lately, those tastings have numbered more than 100 beers from 50ish breweries.

Brewfest has been a multi-site affair in recent years, with some tastings held in an 1890s mill while others happen at popular waterfront restaurants. Live music at all spots, with genres running from indie and bluegrass to funk and old-school rock. When you need a break, there are plenty of interesting diversions in St. Michaels—museums, shops, galleries, and a throwback ice cream parlor among them.

TIP JAR: By signing on for VIP status, you'll likely get to go for a cruise aboard a replica 1930s steam ferry, *The Patriot*, outfitted with tasting stations staffed by brewery owners and brewmasters.

Tourism info: St. Michaels Business Association and/or Talbot County (Md.) Tourism

MID-ATLANTIC SEA GLASS AND COASTAL ARTS FESTIVAL

Early June in Lewes, Del.
Region: Lower Delaware

The Delmarva Peninsula's second big warm-weather celebration of sea glass and its associated arts happens in the coastal town of Lewes. The Mid-Atlantic Sea Glass and Coast Arts Festival usually features 50-plus artisans from all over the Mid-Atlantic region (and often beyond as well). Special collections from notable artists might well be on display in gallery fashion for the weekend.

The festivities will include a bevy of crafts and other activities for children. Authors will be on hand to chat with guests, sign books, and perhaps even offer help with glass-shard identification questions about your collection. Live music and food trucks will be in the lineup as well. That music lineup in recent years has ranged from bluegrass to classic rock.

In a bonus, admission gives you access to the myriad properties managed by the excellent Lewes Historical Society. Take a break from ogling that sea glass by wandering through notable old homes, visiting a maritime museum, checking out an old lifesaving station, and more. Go to Canalfront Park, too—it's like an outdoor museum, full of historical tidbits, including the Lightship Overfalls.

Tourism info: Lewes Chamber of Commerce and/or Southern Delaware Tourism

St. George's Blues Fest

Early June in Delaware City, Del.
Region: Upper Delaware

Not so long ago, the country store in Saint Georges, Del. was just that—a ramshackle stop where locals in a town of a couple hundred people would stop to pick up chips, sodas, subs, and the like. But new owners came along a dozen or so years ago with quite a different kind of place in mind—they wanted to team up with the Diamond State Blues Society and transform the place into a roadhouse juke joint.

Mission accomplished: Today, Saint Georges Country Store is a cherished destination for roots-music aficionados from all over the Delmarva Peninsula, not to mention Philadelphia and Baltimore. The project involved quite the leap of faith, considering that as near as anyone can tell, Saint Georges hadn't had a business with a liquor license since back in the early 1800s. But as of this writing the store has live shows several nights a week, many headlined by top names on the national blues, zydeco, and rockabilly circuits. To make matters even better, the store doubles as a restaurant specializing in Cajun dishes

This summer weekend is the club's showcase annual event—a two-day outdoor extravaganza at nearby Fort DuPont State Park, just below Delaware City. Top regional acts and national headliners perform each day. Harmonica workshops and other fun extras have been part of the deal in recent years. Bring chairs, blankets, and a canopy if you like. Needless to say, there will be food and beer vendors aplenty. Be sure to spend some time in the jam-happy "Sessions Tent," where random collections of musicians from various bands will come and go as moved by their musical muses.

Tourism info: New Castle County (Del.) Tourism

SMYRNA AT NIGHT

June in Smyrna, Del.
Region: Upper Delaware

As welcome-to-summer parties go, Smyrna at Night falls into the kick-out-the-jams category. Recent years have seen twenty-plus groups performing on multiple stages set up throughout the historic downtown. There will be non-musical fun, too, with family activities and lots of vendors showing off arts and crafts. Organizers seem to pay special attention to food truck abundance, with 15 or so mobile meal-and-libation stands on the menu. One more thing: Admission is free.

When you need a break from the music, get in touch with stories from days gone by at the Smyrna Museum. Two buildings there date to the 1700s. And be sure while wandering to check out the town's Opera House, as that venerable building dates to 1869 and hosted speeches and performances by the likes of Frederick Douglass, leading suffragettes, and the famous circus dwarf General Tom Thumb before becoming a movie house in the 1900s. A fire tore through the Opera House in 1948, but it was restored to much of its former glory back in 2003.

Tourism info: Kent County (Del.) Tourism

OCEAN CITY AIR SHOW

Mid-June in Ocean City, Md.
Region: Lower Eastern Shore of Maryland

Heads up! This overhead flight of fancy is a tradition in this oceanfront resort around the time of Father's Day. The aerial lineup is always stellar, with top billing often going to either the U.S. Air Force Thunderbirds or the U.S. Navy Blue Angels. Commando parachute teams and high-tech search-and-rescue units have performed in recent years. Lots of historic old planes will be soaring over the sand, too.

The action happens above the "Drop Zone" area, with the stretch of beach between 12th and 20th streets outfitted with exhibits, interactive displays, and spectator seating. You could try and play cheapskate by watching from a distance, but that's going to be a hassle—no chairs are allowed on the boardwalk, for instance. Instead, most folks opt for a ticket that puts them at the equivalent of a 50-yard-line seat at a football game. Ticket buyers can come and go from the zone with a wristband, so the joys of the boardwalk will be open to you, and you'll be able to make it down to Thrasher's to buy Dad a bucket of fries.

TIP JAR: VIP options here include shade availability and some catering in the "Flight Line Club;" seats in an elevated "Skybox;" or the full-on "Penthouse option," 10 floors up and approaching eye-level with some of the acrobatic action.

Tourism info: Ocean City (Md.) Tourism

BERLIN BATHTUB RACES

Mid-June in Berlin, Md.
Region: Lower Eastern Shore of Maryland

Let us count the ways Berlin ranks as a star attraction on this part of Delmarva. It's got a prime location, just inland from Ocean City. It's got a Hollywood claim to fame as the backdrop for Julia Roberts and Richard Gere in "Runaway Bride." And it's been on a revitalization roll in the 21st century—*Budget Travel* magazine dubbed it "America's Coolest Small Town" a few years back.

One more: The populace has a wacky streak that plays out in events like these Bathtub Races. Laughter rules the streets here when local teams show up with vehicles assembled by tacking axles, wheels, and steering mechanisms onto the underside of antique tubs. Race night is traditionally a Friday, and the competition unfolds with one member of each team, perhaps decked out in a ridiculous old bathing costume, occupying a steering position in the tub, while the other does sprinting duty as a pusher.

The course runs down Main Street, where sidewalks will be packed five or six deep with laughing, cheering onlookers. In the beginning, this evening of wacky midsummer madness consisted of the races and that's about it, but it's more of a block party now, stretching from afternoon into nighttime.

TIP JAR: Keep an eye out for the vintage red racing tub that started this tradition off back in 1989. Created by five-time race champion Jesse Turner of the old Berlin Shoe Box, it now ranks as a cherished local heirloom. They'll probably have it on display outdoors on race night.

Tourism info Berlin Chamber of Commerce and/or Worcester County (Md.) Tourism

THE FIREFLY MUSIC FESTIVAL

June in Dover, Del.
Region: Upper Delaware

Year in and year out the lineup of 80-plus performers at the three-day Firefly extravaganza in Dover is chock full of rising-star artists on the cusp of making a big name for themselves. From hip-hop to soul to rock and beyond, pretty much every genre gets a set or two in the spotlight. The timing here is a bit of guess-work on my part. The event was a June affair for many years, then switched temporarily to a fall slot during the pandemic. As this book was going to press organizers announced Firefly would return in 2024 after a one-year hiatus, but they haven't announced which month they're going with, so I'm basically guessing by putting it in the summer chapter.

There are two ways to join the 50,000 or so fans who come to Firefly every year. One is to go all-in and pitch a tent for the long weekend at The Woodlands, the 105-acre festival site. Firefly's organizers claim that they run the largest camping event on the East Coast. The recent addition of a permanent shower house might make the experience a tad more glamorous.

Single-day tickets are available, too. When you need a break from the bands, Firefly offers other activities—in recent years, those options have included an arcade tent full of games, a design-your-own shoe station, a silent rave called The Thicket, and a beer bar powered by Delaware's own Dogfish Head Brewery. Music-oriented panel discussions and talks will probably be on the bill, too.

Tourism info: Kent County (Del.) Tourism

SEPARATION DAY

Mid-June in New Castle, Del.
Region: Upper Delaware

Every year, the people of Delaware set aside a summer Saturday to celebrate the fact that they do not live in Pennsylvania. Everyone is welcome, even Pennsylvanians! Before you go thinking that this event is rooted in some endemic dislike for that larger state north of Delaware, a little history reminder is in order. Delaware started its colonial life as the southernmost piece of Pennsylvania. William Penn himself gave the town of Lewes its name. In the momentous summer of 1776, with the spirit of independence on the rise, the assembly of the "Lower Counties of Pennsylvania" voted unanimously to deny obedience not just to the rule of the English King George III, but also to the authority of the Penn family and its colony.

Held in history-laden New Castle on the Delaware River, the Separation Day festivities usually start on Friday evening with a party on the old courthouse square. The main event is Saturday, with a parade kicking things off, followed by carnival-style rides, music, food, libations, and a big "Vintage Market." There might be military re-enactors and other living-history touches as well.

The not-Pennsylvania party traditionally closes with a fireworks show. Plus, the New Castle Sailing Club traditionally puts on a regatta to coincide with this festive weekend, so the riverfront scenery should be even more spectacular than usual.

Tourism info: New Castle County (Del.) Tourism

DRINK MARYLAND

Mid-June in Centreville, Md.
Region: Upper Eastern Shore

This celebration of Free-State goodness serves up a one-stop sampling of the state of the art when it comes to Maryland-made wine, beer, and spirits. In recent years, the event has featured the handiwork of 10ish wineries, 10ish distilleries, and half a dozen or so breweries. After purchasing a tasting glass, you'll make the rounds of pouring stations and enjoy other diversions along the way—food vendors, artisan displays, and live music among them.

The setting is gorgeous and appropriate. "Lawyer's Row" is a run of early 20th century Beaux Arts-style offices that stand in the shadow of the venerable Queen Anne's County Courthouse, the oldest such building in Maryland still being used for its original purpose.

Trivia item: When that courthouse went up in the 1790s, the Maryland spirits business was just starting to boom for the first time, thanks to some entrepreneurially savvy Scots Irish immigrants who started churning out rye whiskey to replace the British rum that fell into short supply in those post-Revolutionary years of trading tensions between the U.S. and England. Maryland-style rye would remain a big deal all the way up until Prohibition.

Tourism info (Centreville is near the border of two counties.)

Queen Anne's County (Md.) Tourism
Kent County (Md.) Tourism

FIVE FIRE COMPANY CARNIVALS
Various locations in June, July, and August

Wandering these old-time carnivals will feel like strolling through a Norman Rockwell painting. The sights, smells, and sounds of childhood days gone by will fill the air—think Tilt-a-Whirl rides, merry-go-rounds, shooting games, ring tosses, and those oh-so-elusive stuffed-animal prizes. Think, too, about hot dogs, hamburgers, ice cream, cotton candy, and—around here anyway—oyster fritters.

Firehouse carnivals embody all-American traditions on a deeper level, too, as they're rooted in a regional culture that places a high premium on community self-help and volunteerism. In Chincoteague, Va., the carnival was launched in the 1920s after a devastating fire left firefighting volunteers determined to get better equipment. Similarly, the carnival in Hebron, Md.—launched during those same 1920s—paid for the town's first-ever firehouse. Here are five such summertime carnivals:

Hebron Fireman's Carnival
June through the Independence Day holiday in Hebron, Md.
Region: Lower Eastern Shore of Maryland
        Tourism info: Wicomico County (Md.) Tourism

Wachapreague Fireman's Carnival
Mid-June through Mid-July in Wachapreague, Va.
Region: Eastern Shore of Virginia
        Tourism info: Eastern Shore of Virginia Tourism

Chincoteague Fireman's Carnival

July in Chincoteague, Va.
Region: Eastern Shore of Virginia
        Tourism info: Chincoteague Chamber of Commerce and/
or Eastern Shore of Virginia Tourism

Greensboro Fireman's Carnival

Mid-July in Greensboro, Md.
Region: Upper Eastern Shore of Maryland
        Tourism info: Caroline County (Md.) Tourism

Sharptown Firemen's Carnival

August in Sharptown, Md.
Region: Lower Eastern Shore of Maryland
        Tourism info: Wicomico County (Md.) Tourism

THE RUNNING OF THE BULL

Late June/Early July in Dewey Beach, Del.
Region: Lower Delaware

Quick event summary: Two guys in a cheesy bull costume will chase you down the beach. Really, it works! This inspired bit of wackiness began as a one-off gag. Trying to convince a buddy to join them on a trip to Dewey Beach in the mid- 1990s, some guys promised they would re-create the magic of the famous Running of the Bulls in Pamplona, Spain. They rented a cheesy bull suit, put two guys under it, and had that fake bull chase their buddy down the beach. Thirtysome other people in that group ran in mock terror from the mock bull in year one. The next year, the crowd doubled to 70, and the owner of the famed Starboard bar asked organizers to turn their private fun into a big public event.

The Running of the Bull is now a daylong affair that draws thousands. The main afternoon run follows a generous window that begins in late morning so that folks have plenty of time to fuel up with drinks. There will be live music. There will be swell people-watching, as silly hats and crazy costumes abound. Come mid-afternoon, everyone leaves the Starboard to cross busy Route 1 with help from traffic cops. At the beach, a mock matador does battle with a mock bull.

Then that bull runs the beach in pursuit of revelers doing their best to feign looks of terror while sprinting past sun-bathers who may or may not have a clue what's going on.

Afterward, it's back to the Starboard for more revelry. One bartender quoted in a newspaper article a few years back put it this way: "I remember thinking [at first that] it was all absolutely insane. But at the same time, I couldn't help but think how absolutely wonderful it was. A full day of total, reckless abandonment. We all need more days like that."

TIP JAR: If you want the kids or grandkids to experience this insanity without all the alcohol that flows during and after the main run, there has been a morning Running of the Bull in recent years geared especially to families.

Tourism info: Southern Delaware Tourism

NEW CASTLE COUNTY ICE CREAM FESTIVAL

Late June in Wilmington, Del.
Region: Upper Delaware

If you have a pulse, you probably start craving ice cream about two seconds after the first blast of summer heat arrives. This festival at Rockwood Park in northeast Wilmington will satisfy that urge in home-grown style, with at least half a dozen local vendors serving up their sweet scoops in a full-on festival setting on a Saturday in June.

The Ice Cream Festival is kid-friendly through and through. Face painters, stilt walkers, and costumed characters will likely be wandering the grounds. Local cultural institutions will get in on the act, too, demonstrating old-school yarn spinning, basket weaving, and blacksmithing. The Delaware Astronomical Society has put on "solar viewings" in the past. There will be music, food, and vendors. In recent years, the festival has closed with a big fireworks show at dusk.

Be sure to wander the park, which covers 72 acres set around the historic Rockwood Mansion, a Rural Gothic Revival gem that dates to the 1850s. Tours of the mansion will be available, and the six-acre gardens will be open for wandering.

Tourism info: New Castle County (Del.) Tourism and/or Wilmington (Del.) Tourism

TWO STEAM ENGINE EXTRAVAGANZAS

The Tuckahoe Steam and Gas Show
Early/Middle July in Easton, Md.
Region: Upper Eastern Shore of Maryland

The Old Time Wheat Threshing, Steam, and Gas Engine Show
Early August in Federalsburg, Md.
Region: Upper Eastern Shore of Maryland

Life on the Delmarva Peninsula took a big turn toward modern times as the Age of Steam arrived. The speed and size of the smoke-belching ships that began crisscrossing the Chesapeake and Delaware bays in the 1800s brought big-city tourists onto the peninsula and opened up new markets for canneries and seafood processing houses. In our agricultural heartland, powerful new tractors and threshing machines delivered big boosts to farm productivity.

Those steamy days come back to life at this pair of summer events on the Upper Eastern Shore. You'll see a bevy of steam-powered tractors bouncing on dirt roads. You'll see wheat threshing and saw-milling and blacksmithing and more. Living history performers and craftspeople will be doing their part to bring the past to life as well.

Both events will have a similar vibe—the music of choice will be bluegrass and country gospel. Outdoor church services will kick things off on Sundays. Days at the Tuckahoe show—it's the bigger of the two—usually begin with a solemn flag-raising ceremony and end with a Grand Parade of All Old Equipment. They'll probably have a restored line-shaft-driven machine shop up and running. Visit the on-site Rural Life Museum to get in touch with more stories of life in times gone by. A cool model of the old steamship *Dorchester* is on display there.

The work of a wonderfully named nonprofit, the "Eastern Shore Thresherman," the Federalsburg show is the smaller of the two. Held in early August, it's located a little deeper out in the countryside, between Denton and Federalsburg.

Tuckahoe event tourism info: Talbot County (Md.) Tourism. Old-Time Threshing tourism info: Caroline County (Md.) Tourism

TWO LADYBUG MUSIC FESTIVALS

June and July: One in Milford, Del. and one in Wilmington, Del.
Region: Upper Delaware

The organizers of these two music festivals didn't set out to create the country's "largest celebration of women in music." In 2010, stay-at-home mom Gayle Dillman wanted to help her daughter grow as a musician by arranging for her to play a live concert, only to find that venues and opportunities for the underage set were few and far between. Next thing Dillman knew, she and her daughter's music teacher, Jeremy Hebbel, were renting a venue and putting on a "Rock Showcase" for kids in suburban Yorklyn.

A hundred people showed up to see that first show, and the organizers had found a new passion in life. Dillman and Hebbel soon launched Gable Music Ventures to develop and promote not just kid-focused shows, but all kinds of concerts. Ladybug, which takes its name from the official state bug of Delaware, started out small—first-year attendance was 300—but it has since evolved into a rising star on the Delaware summer- events calendar, with attendance up over 10,000 in at least one recent year.

Organizers strive to bring in the region's best female-led rock, soul, and pop bands, with performances on multiple stages set up once a year in downtown Wilmington, Del. and once a year farther south in Milford, Del. Think of it as a distaff-focused alternative to the more famous Firefly Festival held in Dover every year. Cheaper, too: As of this writing, all shows were free.

The main attraction will be the onstage talent, of course, but Ladybug takes pride in advancing the cause at hand off stage as well as on. Pay attention to backstage scenes and you will see that about three in four event staffers are women, including sound engineers, lighting technicians, and other specialists, all working gigs usually filled by men.

The events have moved around the calendar in recent years, thanks to COVID and other factors. In the year this book was published, the Wilmington Ladybug was in May and the Milford affair was in late July, but you'll have to check to see if that sticks.

Wilmington Ladybug info: Wilmington (Del.) Tourism
Milford Ladybug info (the town straddles two counties):
Southern Delaware Tourism (Sussex County)
Kent County (Del.) Tourism

NANTICOKE RIVERFEST

Mid-July in Seaford, Del.
Region: Lower Delaware

How many chances in life do you get to plop yourself down in an inner tube and float down a warm and lazy river en route to a downtown street festival? In Seaford, Del., that opportunity arises once a year. To join that signature "Float-In," you'll park your car near the festival site and take a shuttle over to a launch location. There, you'll waddle into the history-laden waters of the Nanticoke and let the current do all the work as you and your tube meander around a bend or two en route to the heart of old Seaford.

The downtown here has a rich history. Steamboats used to land at the spot where your tubing trip will come to an end. Harriet Tubman walked from this same spot up the hill that leads into downtown while in the midst of conducting a dramatic Underground Railroad escape. The block party along nearby High Street will have a small-town feel, with the attractions in recent years including beauty pageants, talent contests, a dunking booth, a rubber ducky race, a big car show, a vendor-filled "Artist Alley," live music, food vendors, kids' activities, and more. Be sure to visit the Seaford Museum during the festival to get a feel for the stories this place has to tell.

TIP JAR: Folks who bring pre-inflated inner tubes will pay a small fee to participate in the Float- In. Buying a new tube or having one inflated on-site will be doable, too, for a larger fee.

Tourism info: Southern Delaware Tourism

DELAWARE STATE FAIR

Middle/Late July in Harrington, Del.
Region: Upper Delaware

The Delaware State Fair is a big-time event full of small-town joys. More than 300,000 people throng to this 10-day midsummer extravaganza in Harrington, a town of 3,500. Glitzy concerts by top national country and pop acts are a big part of the draw, but so, too, are moments of timeless Americana—holding baby chicks in your hands, hopping aboard classic carnival rides, and gawking at livestock displayed in old-school 4-H-style fashion.

You might get to watch the kids or grandkids feed a giraffe or ride a camel. You'll snap pictures of them climbing fire equipment at the Touch a Truck display. You'll cheer with them as contestants rumble by in the big pig races. Ice cream, caramel corn, fries—it's a junk food paradise.

The notion of starting a fair in Harrington dates to a conversation among locals gathered around a potbelly stove at a railroad station in 1919. The first edition of their brainchild unfolded on 30 acres and turned a profit of $43.90, mostly from admission fees to harness races and a "Big Motorcycle Race." Nowadays, the fairgrounds cover more than 300 acres.

In addition to those big-time musical headliners, the entertainment lineup includes lots of homegrown talent, from small community bands to Nanticoke Indian dancers and more. On most nights, the fair closes with a fireworks show at dusk. If you want to enjoy something that was on the schedule at that first-ever fair a century ago, keep an eye out for harness racing, which usually happens as part of the "Governor's Day" festivities.

Tourism info: Kent County (Del.) Tourism

PLEIN AIR EASTON ART FESTIVAL & COMPETITION

Mid-July in Easton, Md.
Region: Upper Eastern Shore of Maryland

One of the most prestigious competitions of its kind in the county, Plein Air Easton brings 60ish top artists into Talbot County, Md. for a week. Their mission? Paint masterpieces while standing out in the "plein air" in front of subjects that range from ramshackle old barns to historic small-town storefronts and pretty waterfront vistas.

Your mission is to hang out with this artsy set during the event and its associated parties. At a ticketed Collector's Preview and awards gala—it's usually held on a Friday night—the works these "official" festival artists create will be the main attraction. In the days that follow, those works go on display in an exhibit free and open to all.

Lots of artists outside that official group get in on the creative fun as well. A Quick Draw competition puts nearly 200 painters in front of easels on the streets of downtown Easton. They have two hours to go from first stroke to finish line, and you can join the throng of visitors who crowd the streets during that window, looking over the shoulders of artists as they work. Those Quick Draw works then go up on display in a makeshift outdoor "gallery." A gallery-hopping downtown block party will likely be in the mix as well.

Thanks to an array of community groups, arts nonprofits, and those local galleries, you'll be able to attend demonstrations, workshops, and lectures throughout the week. At an Artisan's Market, you can check out the work of regional artists working in other media—jewelry, pottery, metalwork, and more.

If you want to take home a work by one of those juried artists, get tickets to the Collector's Preview event—do it early, as the party always sells out. Once there, you'll get to enjoy food and libations, but don't get to dawdling and don't be indecisive—artworks sell during the 90-minute sales window at a rate of one every 45 seconds.

Feel-good bonus: The event raises a boatload of money for good local causes.

Tourism info: Talbot County (Md.) Tourism

CHINCOTEAGUE PONY SWIM

Late July in Chincoteague, Va.
Region: Eastern Shore of Virginia

This one is on a lot of bucket lists, and why not? How many chances do we get in life to watch cherished childhood memories come to life? Before doing a little research, I assumed that Pony Swim Week became a thing only after Marguerite Henry published *Misty of Chincoteague* in the 1940s. That book became a children's classic and then a Hollywood movie, helping the ponies of Chincoteague to earn a cherished spot in the hearts of generations of American children.

It turns out, however, that this tradition dates back centuries, not decades. Historians say that the earliest mention of a pony swim dates to 1835. Even at that point, the event ranked as an "ancient" local custom. Its modern incarnation dates to the 1925 launch of a volunteer fire company in the wake of a terrible fire in downtown Chincoteague. The fledgling fire company auctioned off a few ponies that year during a summertime carnival.

In one short decade later, it grew into a multi-day extravaganza drawing crowds of 25,000.

Fair warning: It's gonna be crowded. Throughout this week, you will likely encounter long lines, annoying traffic, and big crowds. Parking will be a pain—expect to take some shuttle buses. Hotels will be pricey and available only for extended stays of several days. If you want the best views, you'll need to plan months in advance, reserving spots on boats for the swim and special tours to other pony excursions.

The event is a weeklong affair. On Saturday and Sunday, local "Saltwater Cowboys" round up the wild ponies that live out in the marsh on Assateague Island and herd them into two different corrals. At daybreak on Monday, ponies from the northern corral are led on a beach walk to join their compadres in the southern corral.

Wednesday brings the big swim—the ponies paddle across Assateague Channel during a no-current "slack tide" and clamber onto Chincoteague Island. Prime viewing spots are at such a premium—again, charter boat slots are sold out months in advance—that the swim is broadcast live on a supersized TV screen in Veterans Memorial Park. After a rest, the ponies parade over to the carnival grounds, where the auction unfolds on Thursday morning.

That auction serves an ecological purpose in addition to a fundraising one, by keeping the size of the herd at a manageable level where ponies have enough room to roam and food to eat. Proceeds also help pay for veterinary care. Watch during the auction for "Buy Back" ponies—these foals are destined to be returned to the wild on Assateague Island. What the winning bidder gets is a chance to name the pony. These often rank among the highest-priced items.

TIP JAR: During Pony Swim Week, the downtown Island Theatre shows the 1960s Hollywood rendition of *Misty of Chincoteague* on several occasions. Get there early if you want a good seat.

Tourism info: Chincoteague Chamber of Commerce and/ or Eastern Shore of Virginia Tourism

SMITH ISLAND CAMP MEETING

Late July/Early August on Smith Island, Md.
Region: Lower Eastern Shore of Maryland

For two centuries, faithful Christians have embarked on annual pilgrimages to storied islands in the middle of the Chesapeake Bay, looking to nourish their souls and refresh their faith. By most accounts, this gathering of the Methodist faithful convened for the first time in 1887, which is when a sparkling new meeting "grounds" went up in the Smith Island town of Ewell, where this midsummer meeting has been held on those grounds every year since.

But the story of Methodist camp meetings on Smith Island goes back much further, probably to the earliest days of the so-called Second Great Awakening, when a powerful new faith spread like wildfire among the working-class people of the Delmarva Peninsula. The historical record has camp meetings being held on nearby Tangier Island, Va. in about 1808; the first gatherings here on Smith Island probably happened around then, too.

There are two reasons why modern-day visitors might want to make a pilgrimage to Smith Island during the Camp Meeting window in late July and early August. The first is the obvious one, to seek peace and renewal through the practice of faith and reflection in a timeless place chock full of God's beauty and bounty. (While a Methodist-organized affair, the meeting is very much open to folks from other denominations and faith traditions.)

The second reason is to immerse yourself in history. The crowds that attend services during the modern-day meeting—sessions are usually held every evening, Monday through Saturday, and several times on Sunday—may not equal the historical numbers from years gone by, but echoes of that past will be strong nonetheless.

Back in the 1800s, people flocked to meetings like this by the thousands, traveling from as far away as Baltimore and Norfolk. The name "camp" meeting comes from the way those visitors stayed in tents and "cottages" that were more like tents with a bit of added structural oomph. At one point, scores of those cottages surrounded the main "tabernacle" here. Learn more about this history by including the Smith Island Cultural Center on your itinerary. The tabernacle is still there, set between a stately old church and a ramshackle Little League field. The floor under that tabernacle is still made of wood shavings, and the benches remain simple, backless affairs. Air conditioning? Don't be ridiculous.

One other bonus: There is an element of "homecoming" to camp meeting time, as natives who have moved on to the mainland often return to the island during this window to pay homage to their childhood meeting memories. That means visitors like you will have more chances than usual to get in touch with and learn from locals.

Tourism info: Somerset County (Md.) Tourism and/or Smith Island (Md.) Cultural Center

Shore Bets!

SEVEN COUNTY FAIRS
July, August, and September in various locations

These old-school celebrations of our farming traditions are rooted in the "agricultural fairs" of the early 1800s. There will be 4-H-style livestock exhibitions. There will be neighborly competitions over whose produce patch produced the best and biggest vegetables. And there will be much more, from wacky greased-pig races and cow-chip tosses to pie-eating contests, tractor pulls, and carnival midways. Below are six county fairs and one other similar event, all on Maryland's Eastern Shore.

There are two more fairs on the annual agenda. See the table of contents to find your way to the Delaware State Fair in July and the Northampton (Va.) Agricultural Fair in October.

Cecil County Fair
Late July in Elkton, Md.
Region: Upper Eastern Shore of Maryland
Two of the traditional draws here are a demolition derby and a professionally sanctioned rodeo.
Tourism info: Cecil County (Md.) Tourism

Kent County (Md.) Fair
Late July in Tolchester Beach, Md.
Region: Upper Eastern Shore of Maryland
In recent years, this event has featured the likes of jousting competitions, archery shows, and even glass-blowing demos.
Tourism info: Kent County (Md.) Tourism

Wicomico County Fair

August in Salisbury, Md.

Region: Lower Eastern Shore of Maryland

Choose a specialty and start practicing if you want to rank as a contender in the watermelon contests. Among the choices: "Speed Eating" and "Seed Spitting."

Tourism info: Wicomico County (Md.) Tourism

Queen Anne's County 4-H Fair

August in Centreville, Md.

Region: Upper Eastern Shore of Maryland

Among the highlights in recent years: a rodeo, a tractor pull, and "dirt sprint" competitions for local race-driver wannabees.

Tourism info: Queen Anne's County (Md.) Tourism

Caroline Dorchester County Fair

August in Denton, Md.

Region: Upper Eastern Shore of Maryland

As in many of the other fairs here, volunteers prepare down-home dinners nightly. Pick the night to visit based on the menu—fried chicken night, crab-cake night, or some other comforting delicacy.

Tourism info: Caroline County (Md.) Tourism and/or Dorchester County (Md.) Tourism

The Great Pocomoke Fair

August in Pocomoke City, Md.

Region: Lower Eastern Shore of Maryland

In a tribute to the glory days of the original Great Pocomoke Fair (1901-1930), you will be able to enjoy harness racing here in addition to a bevy of other fair pleasures.

Tourism info: Worcester County (Md.) Tourism

Worcester County Fair

September in Snow Hill, Md.
Region: Lower Eastern Shore of Maryland
If you are the competitive type, you'll probably be able to sign up here for an egg toss, a tug of war, various eating contests, a limbo battle, a sack race—the list goes on.

Tourism info: Worcester County (Md.) Tourism

BLESSING OF THE COMBINES

Early August in Snow Hill, Md.
Region: Lower Eastern Shore of Maryland

Some other town might put up an argument, but I'd doubt they'd win: The midsummer Blessing of the Combines in downtown Snow Hill, Md. is the region's premier tribute to our hard-working farmers. It's also a ton of fun for kids and kids at heart of all ages.

Your day here will kick off with a fabulous civic parade that reaches its grand finale when a convoy of humongous, brightly colored farm vehicles crosses the Pocomoke River on Washington Street. The sidewalks will be thronged with onlookers. Most everyone will be waving little flags, acting their part in a heartwarming scene of all-American small-town pride.

The title event that follows the parade involves real ministers, so be ready to bow your head and say a few solemn amens while wishing our farmers a safe and prosperous harvest. The big block party after the blessing unfolds in the shadows of several giant combines parked smack dab in the middle of downtown's Greene Street. Yes, you can climb up into the cabs. You can also visit with farm animals, enjoy gospel and country music, shop long rows of food and crafts vendors, enjoy a vintage car show, and more. Don't forget to don one of the stickers volunteers will be handing out here and there—it says, "I Met a Farmer Today!" And when you do, in fact, meet a farmer at the event, be sure to say thanks.

Tourism info: Worcester County (Md.) Tourism

SEVEN PEACH FESTIVALS
August in Various Locations

At events ranging from a giant block party to backroads church socials, you can enjoy down-home sweetness while honoring peach-tree days gone by. Here's a trivia question for those who remember the hit movie "Runaway Bride," with Julia Roberts and Richard Gere: Why is the town in that flick called Hale?

The name is a sly tribute to a tasty slice of Delmarva history. "Runaway Bride" was filmed in Berlin, Md. Berlin, in turn, was once home to an operation called Harrison Farms, which dates to the late 1800s and ranked in the early 1900s as one of the largest fruit-tree operations in the country. The most famous Harrison product was the Hale Peach, named after a family member, G. Hale Harrison.

The story of Delmarva peaches goes back further than that. The first trees probably arrived in Delaware in the 1500s aboard Spanish trading ships. By the 1600s the fruit was so plentiful that farmers were feeding peaches to pigs. The business went into overdrive in the 1800s, when steamboats and railroad lines arrived, allowing local farmers to get the fruits to big-city markets before they spoiled.

Entrepreneurs like Philip Reybold in Delaware City and William Ross in Seaford had launched gargantuan orchards by the time of the Civil War. By 1875, Delaware farmers were producing 6 million baskets of peaches a year. The number of peach trees in the state around that time topped 4 million. It all went south when a disease called "the yellows" appeared and started spreading from one orchard to another. By 1900, there were only 2.4 million peach trees in Delaware. By 1920, that number was down to a paltry 300,000. The disease eventually made its way down into Maryland and wiped out the famed Hale peaches as well.

Nowadays, peaches have only a small role in Delmarva agriculture, but those old peach riches come back front and center every August through the work of the civic groups and volunteers who put on these local festivals.

Middletown Olde-Tyme Peach Festival
Mid-August in Middletown, Del.
Region: Upper Delaware
By far the biggest of the bunch here: This sprawling downtown block party can draw 25,000 attendees if the weather is good. A morning "Peach Parade" kicks things off in sweet fashion.

Tourism info: Middletown (Del.) Historical Society and/or New Castle County (Del.) Tourism

Wyoming Peach Festival

August in Wyoming, Del.

Region: Upper Delaware

This one happens along Railroad Avenue, usually in the first part of the month. Vendors, crafts, contests—maybe find your way to Wyoming Park and walk the shores of Wyoming Lake, too?

Tourism info: Kent County (Del.) Tourism

Berlin Peach Festival

August in Berlin, Md.

Region: Lower Eastern Shore of Maryland

The festival in Berlin takes place on the grounds at the Taylor House Museum in early August—lots of peachy treats, kids activities, music, and more. The nearby downtown area will be hopping as well, with sidewalk vendors and sales.

Tourism info: Berlin Chamber of Commerce and/or Worcester County (Md.) Tourism

Sudlersville Peach Festival

August in Sudlersville, Md.

Region: Upper Eastern Shore of Maryland

This event with crafts, music, and food vendors happens at Godfrey's Farm just west of town in the early part of the month.

Tourism info: Queen Anne's County (Md.) Tourism

Peach Party Weekend

August in Elkton, Md.

Region: Upper Eastern Shore of Maryland

In addition to the title attraction, this event at Milburn Orchards has featured tractor rides, eating competitions, and family-oriented games and races in recent years.

Tourism info: Cecil County (Md.) Tourism

Preston Peach Festival

August in Preston, Md.
Region: Upper Eastern Shore of Maryland
Put on by Preston Bethesda United Methodist Church, this down-home little affair is usually held at the local firehouse.

Tourism info: Caroline County (Md.) Tourism

Antioch Peach Festival

August near Cambridge, Md.
Region: Lower Eastern Shore of Maryland
Another down-home little affair, this one happens at a historic church along the pretty two-lane backroads of the "Neck District," west of Cambridge.

Tourism info: Dorchester County (Md.) Tourism

CHESAPEAKE BAY BALLOON FESTIVAL

Early August in Cordova, Md.
Region: Upper Eastern Shore of Maryland

This photogenic extravaganza drops a colorful array of hot-air balloons into the sprawling farm country northeast of Easton, Md. Get up early if you want to watch a mass ascension at the crack of dawn—or sleep in and bide your time until the early evening ascension.

You'll be able to explore the interior of a partially inflated "Walkabout Balloon." If you act in advance before they sell out, you'll be able to sign up for a full-bore airborne trip over the countryside or choose a "Tethered Ride" that goes 80 or so feet up in the air while attached to terra firma by a strong lifeline. When night comes, a gorgeous "Balloon Glow" illuminates the farmland countryside.

There will be vendors and libations aplenty on the event grounds at Triple Creek Winery. In recent years, the lineup in the "Kids Zone" has included face painting, playground fun, hay-rides, and a "Roaming Railroad." There will probably be presentations by experts on "How Balloons Work," too.

TIP JAR: Be patient with the fact that the balloon rides and the mass ascension events are highly weather dependent. Rain in the forecast and ground-level winds over seven miles an hour can put the kibosh on flight plans. Final decisions may not be made until 45 minutes out from launch time.

Tourism info: Talbot County (Md.) Tourism

DEAD ON THE VINE

Early August in Machipongo, Va.
Region: Eastern Shore of Virginia

This summer night out on Virginia's Eastern Shore is all about the classics. There will be classic rock 'n' roll, courtesy of a Grateful Dead tribute band. There will be classic scenery, as Chatham Vineyards is set along a winding, picturesque creek on the bayside, vaguely near Machipongo. The farm where Chatham operates was first patented by a British settler clear back in 1640. The big brick house is more than 200 years old.

The dinner menu changes from year to year, but whatever mix of salads, grilled meats, fruits, and vegetables get served up when you attend will likely be chock full of locally grown goods. The wine will be homegrown, too, and the beer supplied by a local operation. Come prepared to make yourself comfortable in DIY fashion, with whatever mix of picnic blankets, folding chairs, and other supplies you prefer. In recent years, this has been an advance-ticket-required event, so don't just go showing up at the gate and messing with their dinner counts.

Tourism info: Eastern Shore of Virginia Tourism

OUTDOOR FINE ART AND CRAFT SHOW

Early August in Rehoboth Beach, Del.
Region: Lower Delaware

Outdoor art shows are staples on summer-month calendars in towns all over the Delmarva Peninsula, but few come with the historical pedigree of this one. For starters, that's a matter of geography. Since the earliest days of beach resorts in the late 1800s, Rehoboth has had a reputation as a haven for artists. Some of the famous names involved include Howard Pyle, N.C. Wyeth, and Ethel Pennewill Brown.

Brown was the first to start organizing public exhibits, launching a boardwalk art show in 1928. The Rehoboth Art League dates its history to 1938 and remains a thriving affair, with more than 1,000 members and more than 150 educational sessions offered every year. This particular show dates to the 1970s; it's held on the league's pretty 3.5-acre campus in the planned community of Henlopen Acres on the northwest edge of town. In the early days of the event, works were hung on the snow fencing that surrounds the property. You will probably see a few artists paying homage to that signature display style from the past, while others will opt for more modern-day canopies.

Running across two consecutive weekends, the juried show will probably feature works by 100-plus artists. In addition to gawking at their creations, you'll be able to watch some of them give talks and demonstrations. You'll get to take tours of the league's historic buildings. Kids will find artsy fun in a Children's Studio. Pretty much everyone should enjoy strolling the league's well-kept garden. Food, beer, and live music as well.

Tourism info: Southern Delaware Tourism

BETTERTON DAY

Early August in Betterton, Md.
Region: Upper Eastern Shore of Maryland

A century ago, everyone in the Chesapeake Bay region knew about Betterton Beach. Steamboats stopped at the mouth of the Sassafras River multiple times every day, dropping scads of big-city tourists off to enjoy a beach where stinging jellyfish were scarce and a town where the amenities were abundant. Betterton had 18 hotels and boarding houses in its glory days, along with a dance hall, a movie theater, a casino, a billiards parlor, a bowling alley, and more.

The town is sleepier now, home to just 400 people and a smattering of businesses. But on one summer weekend in August, it reprises its role as a tourist destination by putting on a day of small-town waterfront bliss. In recent years, the festivities have included a Friday-night beach party with music and fireworks. Saturday is the main event, starting with a parade that rolls through town and ends up on a beach that still boasts a bathhouse and 500 feet of boardwalk. More music will be on tap in that sand, along with an array of nearby games, food, and vendors.

Be sure to stroll through town. You'll get a sense along the way for how things used to be in the bits of sweet old Victorian architecture that stand amid an array of more modern condominium buildings. Find your way to the old church that now serves as a community hall to visit the Betterton Heritage Museum, which is full of photos, artifacts, and memorabilia from those glory days.

TIP JAR: If you arrive early enough on Saturday, join in a popular community tradition—a breakfast served up by volunteers at the local American Legion hall.

Tourism info: Kent County (Md.) Tourism

WATERMEN'S APPRECIATION DAY

Early/Middle August in St. Michaels, Md.
Region: Upper Eastern Shore of Maryland

From Native American times up to the present day, the various peoples who've made their home on the Eastern Shore have sustained themselves through good times and bad on the bounty of the Chesapeake Bay and its rivers. That heritage of the region's "watermen" culture is front and center in this annual celebration of fishing, crabbing, and oystering.

Held on the campus of the Chesapeake Bay Maritime Museum, the event includes a boat-docking contest in which workboat captains strive for a winning mix of precision and speed in tight quarters. Locals often dub such affairs the "waterman's rodeo."

Watermen themselves might be among those serving up fresh steamed crabs at the best prices the market will allow. Burgers, hot dogs, corn on the cob, and lots more comfort food will be on the menu, too. Bands perform under the historic Tolchester Beach Bandstand, which once stood at a legendary resort on the Upper Chesapeake Bay. Guided boat rides will probably be available for an extra fee, including cruises aboard historic vessels that are part of the museum's "floating fleet."

Lots of activities for children will be on tap, too, probably including a rowboat competition. The museum's multiple exhibit buildings and expansive outdoor displays will be open to visitors throughout the event.

Tourism info: St. Michaels Business Association and/or Talbot County Tourism

PIRATES AND WENCHES FANTASY WEEKEND

Mid-August in Rock Hall, Md.
Region: Upper Eastern Shore of Maryland

Dig out the eye patches. Unpack the puffy-sleeved shirts. These three days of pirate fun happen in a fishing town set in a remote corner of the upper Chesapeake Bay. The festivities usually get started on Friday evening with sea chanties and rum tastings at a local watering hole.

Come Saturday and Sunday, it's all pirates, all the time. Downtown Rock Hall will be transformed into a stage set for

"Merriment on Main Street," with pirate performers and pirate-themed entertainments. You should be able to sign on for the costume contests and kids activities. You'll be able to eat plenty of grub and drink a little grog. Head back out to the waterfront if you want to watch the decorated dinghy contest—one of the prizes in a recent year went to the "Scurviest Crew." There has been a Pirate Beach Party in recent years, too, and a big Buccaneer's Ball where the King and Queen win their crowns in pirate-prom fashion. If you have young pirate wannabes in your life, this should be right up their alley. There will probably be things like storytelling sessions, mermaid meet-and-greets, puppet shows, and face painting on the agenda.

Tourism info: Kent County (Md.) Tourism

DELMARVALOUS FESTIVAL

Mid-August in Salisbury, Md.
Region: Lower Eastern Shore of Md.

This "folklife festival" celebrating numerous aspects of Delmarva culture is put on by the first-rate Ward Museum of Wildfowl Art, home to one of the world's finest collections of hunting decoys. A bunch of top decoy artists will be on hand, competing in a "Chesapeake Challenge."

But the event has a broader scope, too. The museum and its grounds will be dotted with local artists, craftspeople, and cultural groups. A Folklife Area will celebrate various local traditions. In past years, the demos planned there have included sandcastle making, fly fishing, distilling, hydroponic farming, rug making, mushroom harvesting, and, of course, decoy carving. There will no doubt be new additions to the agenda for the year that you attend.

Be sure to wander the exhibit galleries and take the time to learn about the Ward brothers of Crisfield, Md.—that's how this local institution got its name. Nearby is pretty City Park, where you will find the fun little Salisbury Zoo.

Tourism info: Wicomico County (Md.) Tourism

GROOVE CITY CULTURE FEST

Mid-August in Cambridge, Md.
Region: Lower Eastern Shore

For much of its history, Cambridge (aka "Groove City") had two "main streets" running parallel to one another, just a block apart. Race Street was the commercial corridor for whites, while Pine Street served the same function for blacks. The latter stretch is mostly quiet and residential nowadays, but it's full of music, arts, food, and more during this event celebrating in thoroughly modern ways the African-American stories from days gone by that have earned Pine Street a spot on the National Register of Historic Places.

The first free black to move here did so in the early 1800s, so this has likely been a continuously occupied African-American neighborhood since Thomas Jefferson was president. In the 1960s Pine Street was the center of a nationally significant chapter in the Civil Rights movement. In the 1930s, the community had a homeownership rate approaching 90 percent. Entrepreneurship is another key theme, as dozens of family-run businesses occupied parts of the homes here in the early and middle 1900s. Pine Street was a well-known stop on the chitlin' circuit, too, with multiple venues hosting an incredible mix of musical talent—from Ella

Fitzgerald to James Brown and just about everyone in between.

That last bit is a focus at this Culture Fest, which has been drawing big crowds, thanks in part to the way organizers have been booking first-rate throwback soul and go-go stars as headliners. Expect plenty of dancing in the streets. Vendor tents and food trucks will line four or five blocks. Church ladies will be serving down-home suppers. You might even be able to try "yock," a noodle-based dish with meat or seafood and a spicy sauce that ranks as a little-known old-time culinary specialty in the region.

TIP JAR: If you want to take a deeper dive into the history while you're there, search for "Pine Street Walking Tour" at the Dorchester County Tourism website.

Tourism info: Dorchester County (Md.) Tourism and/or Groove City Black Heritage

CAROLINE SUMMERFEST

Late August in Denton, Md.
Region: Upper Eastern Shore of Maryland

Thankfully, the civic powers that be in Denton nowadays are much better at throwing parties than their predecessors in prior centuries. Around the time of the Civil War, a celebration of Independence Day went horribly wrong when some homemade bottle rockets (fueled with kerosene) landed in a warehouse and set off a blaze that destroyed several blocks full of businesses. In fact, that's one reason why the pretty downtown here is so full of buildings from the late 1800s.

Summerfest has been a local tradition for more than 30 years. To properly plan a fashion statement, you will need to check in advance, as Summerfest adopts a new theme every year—it might be Hollywood one year, the beach another, and superheroes the one after that. Lots of vendors and stores decorate accordingly—and lots of regular folks dress the part as well.

Bring comfortable shoes, as this "block" party covers a whole bunch of blocks— from the courthouse at First Street clear up to Fourth Street. In recent years, that wandering has taken festival goers past multiple music stages, a car show, street performers (whose ranks have included a local belly-dance troupe), a sandcastle display, a climbing wall, model train layouts, and more vendors than you'll have time for. If you are a paddling type, consider the "Rivah Run," a two-mile paddling event with a poker-run twist.

Tourism info: Caroline County (Md.) Tourism

THE AUGUST QUARTERLY

Late August in Wilmington, Del.
Region: Upper Delaware

The nation's oldest continuous celebration of black culture and faith serves up gospel music, storytellers, and family-friendly activities in downtown Wilmington's little Tubman Garrett Park, which actually occupies a couple big slices of African American history. It stands right next to the Market Street bridge—an earlier incarnation of that structure was the site of a dangerous passage in one of the most dramatic escapes in the Underground Railroad career of Harriet Tubman. A statue depicting Tubman alongside Wilmington-based Underground Railroad hero Thomas Garrett is the centerpiece of the park.

A more modest marker stands nearby, introducing another strand of African-American history—this park is the modern-day home of the "August Quarterly," which used to be known as the "Big Quarterly." The first such gathering in the summer of 1813 was organized by the Rev. Peter Spencer, a monumental figure in the days when the black churches first broke free from white oversight to operate on their own, even in slavery times. The event soon grew into a meeting of black Methodists from all over the Mid-Atlantic region.

Nowadays, the August Quarterly is a celebration of history, faith, and religious freedom. Various events unfold over the course of a full week, with the main event coming on that last Sunday. The array of gospel music featured runs from the best local church choirs performing traditional standards to popular regional and national acts whose styles are all over the map. Vendors, storytellers, food stands, and children's activities fill Tubman-Garrett Park as well.

Tourism info: Wilmington (Del.) Tourism

HARRINGTON HERITAGE DAY

Late August in Harrington, Del.
Region: Upper Delaware

Hard to believe, but this celebration set in the farming heartland of Delmarva takes place on land that was once chock full of trees. When Europeans first arrived, a vast forest covered much of Kent and Sussex counties.

Those trees were in the process of disappearing by the time a tavern went up here in the 1780s, turning Harrington into commercial crossroads, with stagecoaches rolling through and farmers riding in to sell produce. That agricultural activity went into overdrive when the railroad arrived in 1856, sparking the development of canneries. Later, garment factories were a big thing.

This annual celebration of that history traditionally kicks off with a small-town parade, which leads into a day of live music and family activities. Visit a trio of little museums devoted to local history. Shop and chat with craftspeople displaying their wares. Join in a blessing of the combines. There will likely be face painting and pony riding available for the younger set. Fireworks have been a part of the show in some recent years.

Tourism info: Kent County (Del.) Tourism

CHAPTER THREE:
FALL EVENTS

TWO SKIPJACK RACES

Deal Island Skipjack Races
Early September in Deal Island, Md.
Region: Lower Eastern Shore of Maryland

Choptank Heritage Skipjack Race
Late September in Cambridge, Md.
Region: Lower Eastern Shore of Maryland

The remote watermen's community of Deal Island has been through its share of changes since the first rendition of this event in 1959, but it's still a place where the threads tying our 21st century present with Delmarva days gone by remain uncommonly strong. You'll see that for yourself during this three-day Labor Day weekend festival highlighted by a race of old-school sailing skipjacks.

Deal Island was originally called "Devil's Island" because it housed some unsavory characters early on, so it's ironic that one of the strongest of those cultural threads involves the inter-twining of watermen and religion. In the early 1800s, this was home base for Rev. Joshua Thomas, the legendary "Parson of the Islands" who traveled among dozens of island pulpits aboard a log canoe called the *Methodist*. You can pay your respects by visiting his grave and stopping in the old Joshua Thomas Chapel. Be sure to check out the Skipjack Heritage Museum, too.

The festival usually kicks off on Saturday evening with gospel music at Deal Island Harbor. Things get into gear along the same lines on Sunday morning, with outdoor church services. There will be vendors, kids activities, a car and motorcycle show, and more. Race day is Labor Day Monday, and here, too, things start with a faith-filled gesture—the Blessing of the Fleet. There will likely be a couple of other races for different vessel types, as well as a fishing tournament and a boat-docking competition. An awards ceremony closes things out. (A note for your double-dipping traveling convenience: The next event here, the Hard Crab Derby, traditionally falls on the same weekend in nearby Crisfield.)

The skipjacks gather again in late September on the Choptank River in Cambridge. There is no festival atmosphere here, so expect the focus to be set firmly on those glorious old sailing ships as they emerge from Cambridge Creek in a parade of sail and then set off from the starting line. The shoreline and docks near the Choptank River Lighthouse and the Cambridge Yacht Club offer the best views. Try to be considerate of the scores of photographers who will be out there hoping to capture a little skipjack magic. Fair warning: The race will end well before noon. Maybe plan on lunch in downtown Cambridge, followed by an afternoon excursion to some other site(s)?

Deal Island race tourism info: Somerset County Tourism and/or the Deal Island Chance Lions Club

Cambridge race tourism info: Dorchester County Tourism

THE HARD CRAB DERBY

Early September in Crisfield, Md.
Region: Lower Eastern Shore of Maryland

This Labor Day weekend festival of crabby contests, boat races, carnival rides, and other merriment happens in a town that has every right to proclaim itself the "Crab Capital of the World." If you've never been to Crisfield, it won't take you long to catch on. The water tower is adorned with a humongous blue crab. Street signs bear cute crab icons.

This town is thick with families that trace their roots back many generations, and the Hard Crab Derby is your opportunity to join those locals on the grounds of Somers Cove Marina in a civic celebration of crustacean proportions.There will be lots of traditional festival fare, including a carnival, live music, vendors, and fireworks. Each day's schedule is built around a crabby or maritime headline event. The Miss Crustacean Pageant usually happens on Thursday, followed on Friday by a big crab-cooking contest. The Crab Derby itself—yes, it's an actual race with actual crustaceans—happens on Saturday, along with a crab-picking contest, a big parade, and a sailboat race. A boat-docking competition—aka the watermen's "rodeo"—tops the Sunday schedule. (A note for your double-dipping traveling convenience: The previous event here, the Deal Island Skipjack Races, is quite nearby and traditionally falls on the same weekend.)

Tourism info: Somerset County Tourism

THE JAZZ FUNERAL

Early September in Bethany Beach, Del.
Region: Lower Delaware

If you didn't expect to find a funeral among the fun events in these pages, then you've never been to Bethany Beach on Labor Day Monday. This farewell-to-summer bash borrows from the New Orleans tradition of taking to the streets to mark the passing of loved ones with music, marching, and other bits of joyous remembrance.

Gather with fellow mourners at the north end of the boardwalk and get behind the open casket containing a mannequin dressed up in tribute to dearly departed summertime. Mourners are encouraged to dress for the occasion. Some do that simply by donning black t-shirts or wrapping themselves in a shroud. Others show up in elaborate clerical garb or decked out as the Grim Reaper.

Dixieland-style musicians will strike up a dirge as all you mourners shuffle down the boards toward the downtown Boardwalk Bandstand. Along the way there will be much sobbing and carrying on. Near the bandstand, the tempo of the music will pick up, tunes taking on one extra bounce after another until the entire affair turns as if by magic into a raucous party.

Bonus event: A similar event happens just up the road in Rehoboth Beach. The farewell-to-summer Piping Out Parade there also happens on Labor Day Monday, and there are lots of kazoos involved.

Tourism info: Southern Delaware Tourism

OCEANS CALLING MUSIC FESTIVAL

Late September in Ocean City, Md.
Region: Lower Eastern Shore of Maryland

Will Oceans Calling become the region's next must-see mega-music festival? That question was still up in the air as this book went to press since the first-ever rendition of the event got washed out by a tropical storm, disappointing tens of thousands of fans of Dave Matthews, the Lumineers, Alanis Morissette, and other top-notch acts.

But the lineup for that canceled affair was strong enough to bode well for the future of Oceans Calling. Plus, the company that puts it together has a history of success—they also do the Austin City Limits Music Festival in Texas, the Voodoo Music + Arts Experience in New Orleans, and the Lollapalooza festival in Chicago.

Oceans Calling is planned as a three-day affair featuring 30ish performances on three stages set up in and around the inlet area at the lower end of the Ocean City Boardwalk. That location will put fans within strolling distance of classic beach attractions like the Ocean City Fishing Pier, the old-school Jolly Roger Amusement Park, and countless other joys up and down the boardwalk. Fingers crossed for blue skies and calm winds in the year you decide to go ...

Tourism info: Ocean City (Md.) Tourism and/or Worcester County Tourism

BETHANY BEACH BOARDWALK ARTS FESTIVAL

Early September in Bethany Beach, Del.
Region: Lower Delaware

For more than four decades now, the Boardwalk Arts Festival has lived up to its name by giving folks the chance to peruse artworks while within sight of the ocean waves. About 100 painters, photographers, woodworkers, metal artisans, jewelry makers, glass blowers, and textile artists pass muster with the jury that selects participants.

You will get to meet and talk with many of those creative souls while wandering among tents set up around Bethany's bandstand and along the boardwalk. The price points here will vary as widely as the styles, from small works at $20 or $30 to floor-to-ceiling showstoppers that run up into the thousands.

You'll never be far away from your favorite beach indulgences, whether that's taffy, fries, ice cream, or shops. There will be some live music and some family-friendly art activities, but for the most part you can expect the Boardwalk Arts Festival to be exactly what that name says it is.

Tourism info: Bethany-Fenwick Area Chamber of Commerce and/or Southern Delaware Tourism

FESTIVAL HISPANO

Mid-September in Georgetown, Del.
Region: Lower Delaware

Dive into the region's rich Hispanic culture and heritage at this music-oriented street festival in the seat of Sussex County. You might want to brush up on your Latin dance steps first, as music is the main draw. Organizers bring in big-name national and international touring acts specializing in cumbia, merengue, bachata, norteño, punta, reggaeton, and other styles. Past headliners have included bachata superstar Luis Vargas and the so-called "Kings of Cumbia," Grupo Control.

The event is set along Race Street in the Sussex County seat of Georgetown, long a Southern Delaware stronghold when it comes to Latino population numbers and cultural amenities. Festival Hispano can draw 10,000 or more attendees with the right combination of star power and good weather. Stroll away from the stage and you'll likely find more than 100 vendor tents, many featuring traditional arts and crafts. Local dance troupes show off their steps in street-performer fashion. Local restaurants and community groups go all out preparing traditional street foods.

Launched in the mid-1990s, the festival is the work of a nonprofit group called La Esperanza. Proceeds support community outreach to newly arrived immigrant families as they get acclimated to their Delmarva surroundings.

Tourism info: Southern Delaware Tourism

TWO NATIVE AMERICAN FESTIVALS

The Nanticoke Powwow
Mid-September in Lewes, Del.
Region: Lower Delaware

Native American Festival
Mid-September in Vienna, Md.
Region: Lower Eastern Shore of Maryland

Join the descendants of local Indian tribes as they celebrate their heritage during these outdoor festivals filled with crafts, native foods, music, and dancing.

The Nanticokes were among the first Indian tribes to make contact with European settlers. Captain John Smith of Jamestown, Va. fame was trading with them for beaver pelts back in 1608. The Nanticoke didn't fare very well once their old world took a "New" turn, suffering terribly from European diseases and, later, the loss of land to settlers. Like other tribes in the region, they were gone or dispersed into near invisibility before the Revolutionary War.

But their bloodlines still survive today, and their traditions come to life several times a year. At both these events, you'll enjoy traditional singing and dancing while admiring the work of native craftspeople and learning about cultural traditions.

The Nanticoke Powwow began in Millsboro on the ground of the interesting little Nanticoke Indian Museum, but the big crowds it drew led to a recent move to a larger site in Lewes. It's the largest annual gathering of its kind on Delmarva, with performers representing tribes up and down the Eastern Seaboard—and often from points beyond.

Put on by a Nanticoke band called the Nause-Waiwash, the smaller Vienna event begins with a Grand Entry and the Flag Song featuring native dancers. There will be Native arts, crafts, food, drumming, and more. Here, too, other tribes from around the region will be represented by performers and dignitaries. By the way, the name Nanticoke is a fitting affair—it derives from an Indian word that means "tidewater people."

Tourism info:

Nanticoke Powwow: Southern Delaware Tourism

Native American Festival: Dorchester Co. (Md.) Tourism

OCEAN CITY BIKEFEST

Mid-September in Ocean City, Md.
Region: Lower Eastern Shore of Maryland

Let's get ready to rumble! If your idea of a perfect weekend at the beach includes the roar of motorcycle engines by the thousands, lots of raucous hard rock classics, and a plethora of bikini bike-wash stations along Coastal Highway, then Bikefest needs to be on your September to-do list. Running through a long weekend, its ranks as the biggest annual celebration of motorbike culture on the East Coast.

If past years are a guide, you'll be able to watch stunt shows, meet bike manufacturers, test out new models, admire classic old vehicles, meet celebrity bikers, and much more. Most events happen either down at the Ocean City Inlet or up at the Powell Convention Center. Nearby towns like Salisbury, Snow Hill, and Delmar offer bike-themed events as well.

Wherever you go, food tents vendors abound. Even Delaware's Cape May-Lewes Ferry gets in on the act, offering motorcycle-only trips across the Delaware Bay through the weekend. The event generally showcases top-of-the-line names in classic rock, including such recent headliners as ZZ Top, Cheap Trick, Styx, and KIX.

Depending on how the calendar falls in any given year, Bikefest may land on or near Sept. 11. On those occasions, there will likely be a solemn "Parade of Brothers" cruising down the boardwalk to honor victims of the 9/11 terrorist attacks.

Tourism info: Ocean City Tourism and/or Worcester County (Md.) Tourism

ELKTON FALL FEST

Middle/Late September in Elkton, Md.
Region: Upper Eastern Shore of Maryland

Fall festivals pop up with the simple changing of seasons in our modern times, but their roots are in deeper rhythms of farm family living—as celebrations of harvest times. In Elkton, they do right by those traditions during a weekend party in a downtown thick with Americana stories and Main Street atmosphere. The 1769 Mitchell House at 131 E. Main St. served as a makeshift hospital for wounded soldiers during the Revolutionary War. George Washington passed along Main Street en route to a triumphant encounter at Yorktown. Unlike several neighboring towns that got raided and burned by the British during the War of 1812, the citizens here beat back British attacks on both land and water.

The Fall Fest fun usually begins on Friday evening when Main Street is closed to traffic for a big car show and live music. On Saturday, the festival runs all day with the likes of a Cub Scouts push-cart derby, kids activities galore, and fun memorabilia from days gone by. Who will win this year's Pretty Baby Contest? How about the Voice of Elkton competition?

Local bands perform all day. Craftspeople, artists, and vendors have been told in recent years to have tents up and running by 8am. Usually, the local American Legion offers a one-two punch of funnel cakes and beer. The shops and restaurants along Main Street will no doubt be going all out as well. Be sure to stop at the Historical Society of Cecil County, which always seems to have interesting displays up.

Tourism info: Cecil County (Md.) Tourism

MARYLAND FOLK FESTIVAL IN SALISBURY

September in Salisbury, Md.
Region: Lower Eastern Shore of Maryland

Founded in 1934, the National Folk Festival is the work of the nonprofit National Council for the Traditional Arts, which runs the festival as an itinerant affair, moving from one city to another for three-year runs. The idea is for the national nonprofit to teach locals during that three-year run how to take over and keep the party going. It's worked out according to plan for quite a few towns, and Salisbury is hoping to join their ranks, transitioning into the Maryland Folk Festival in Salisbury as this book was getting finalized.

Here's hoping the local organizers don't miss a beat in that transition. Much of downtown Salisbury was transformed into a festival ground during the event's early years, with multiple performance stages, a folk traditions center, an artisans' market-place, a family activities zone, and more. Look over the music schedules from recent years and you'll catch on to the reason why more than 150,000 people attended one recent festival. Top names in blues, zydeco, rockabilly, bluegrass, and more serve as headliners, but the lineup is also full of stars in lesser known genres—think exotic stuff on the order of Bolivian tinku dancers, Inuit throat singers, and Indian kuchipudi dancers.

Upon arrival, you'll get a program listing performance times and locations. I suggest you put that in your pocket and leave it there. Instead, just wander around and see what you run into. The real fun here is stumbling into performers that wouldn't have made your advance hit list. That's how I found myself enjoying shows I'll long remember—Hawaiian swing music, a Quebecois folk trio, East African soukous, and Balkan tamburitza string music among them.

Tourism info: Downtown Salisbury (Md.) and/or Wicomico County (Md.) Tourism

TAWES CRAB & CLAM BAKE

Mid- to Late September in Crisfield, Md.
Region: Lower Eastern Shore of Maryland

The motto at the largest seafood festival in Maryland pretty
much says it all: "Clams, Crabs, Beer, and Politics." First things
first: 300 bushels of crabs, 8,400 ears of corn, 200 watermelons,
30,000 clams, and who-knows-how-many french fries. That's
what the mostly volunteer team working this event cooked up in
one recent year.

Oddly, the title of largest seafood festival belongs to an
event that happens on a Wednesday—it used to be in July, but recently switched over to September. Lots of regular folks like you
and me line up long before the gates open in hopes of snagging a
shady table at Somers Cove Marina. Others pay extra to reserve a
spot under a tent and get access to a special beer wagon.

You might want to spend a little time in advance study-
ing up on the names and photos of political bigwigs in Maryland.
Somewhere along the line, the Tawes Crab & Clam Bake became
a must-stop schmoozefest for everybody who's anybody among
actual and wannabe elected officials.

The location here is a fitting one, as Crisfield is a town
whose history gives it every right to claim the title "Crab Capital
of the World." The waterfront looks out onto wide Daugherty
Creek, which heads in turn out into the storied Tangier Sound.

Tourism info: Somerset County (Md.) Tourism

EASTON AIRPORT DAY

Late September/Early October in Easton, Md.
Region: Upper Eastern Shore of Maryland

This flight of fancy started by accident. More than a decade ago, the Red Star Pilots Association was holding a private meeting at the Easton Airport on Route 50 just north of town. That event included a formation training exercise in which a fleet of old Yak Warbirds maneuvered in an aerial ballet full of dips and turns in the skies over Talbot County.

Residents and passersby alike figured there must be an air show going on, so they headed over to the airport, looking to get in on the fun. This got the association and the airport and some local pilots to thinking: Hey, why not?

A formation flyover remains a centerpiece of the Easton Airport Day festivities. With more than 25 planes involved, it ranks as one of the largest formation flyovers in the country. You will enjoy some serious wackiness as well, especially when it comes time for the "World Famous Rubber Chicken Drop." Pilots roar over the runway and release a rubber chicken in hopes of hitting a bullseye by landing it in the back of a pickup truck. Some pilots concoct fun, jerry-rigged "chicken launchers" for the occasion. As of this writing, no one has ever nailed that bullseye. Nonetheless, the event has become so popular that it now has its own costumed mascot, Captain Peeps.

While wandering past vendors and food stands on the airport grounds, you'll be able to check out lots of historic and military aircraft. There will likely be quite a display of vintage cars, too. When making fashion decisions for Easton Airport Day, keep in mind that you will probably have the opportunity to climb up into the cockpit of a fighter jet for a photo op. Maybe dig out your best Snoopy scarf and look ready to do battle with the Red Baron?

Tourism info: Talbot County (Md.) Tourism

Two Emancipation Celebrations

Harriet Tubman Emancipation Day
Mid-September near Cambridge, Md.
Region: Lower Eastern Shore of Maryland

Frederick Douglass Day
Late September in Easton, Md.
Region: Upper Eastern Shore of Maryland

These two events celebrate incredible stories from the lives of Eastern Shore natives who lifted themselves from the bonds of slavery and climbed into the top ranks of American heroes.

Young Fred Bailey's journey to freedom got off to a rocky start. The first time the enslaved young man tried to make a run for it in the 1830s, he ended up doing time in jail in Easton, Md. But he survived that ordeal and eventually found his way to freedom, where he would adopt a new name, Frederick Douglass, and become a world-renowned orator, writer, and abolitionist.

The summer of 1849 was a desperate time in the life of Harriet Tubman, too. The death of her owner left her family in Dorchester County, Md. distraught over the chance that some or all of them would be sold off and sent far away to clear out the debts that owner left behind. On Sept. 17, Tubman decided once and for all that the bonds of slavery would not hold her.

She and two brothers ran off, hoping to find a way to freedom in the North. That run failed, as her brothers got cold feet. But the course of Tubman's life was now set: Soon after that, she made her successful run along the Underground Railroad. Later, she would come back and get those brothers.

On a weekend near the anniversary of Tubman's first flight, the Harriet Tubman Underground Railroad Visitor Center outside of Cambridge will likely have park rangers leading kid-friendly sessions and Tubman experts giving talks and leading conversations. Musical and theatrical performances might be on the bill as well.

In and around the Talbot County Free Library at the Easton event in recent years, there has been a parade, a block party with music, and presentations by historians, along with a festival marketplace and a children's village. Check the Douglass Day schedule to see if they are offering walking tours of the nearly Hill Neighborhood, which ranks among the oldest African-American communities in the whole country. Lots of fascinating historical and archeological discoveries have been made there in recent years.

TIP JAR: If you want to explore the lives of these two heroes in more depth, search the internet for the Harriet Tubman Byway and/or the Frederick Douglass Driving Tour of Talbot County. And there's always my book: *Tubman Travels: 32 Underground Railroad Journeys on Delmarva.*

Tourism info:

Tubman event: Dorchester County (Md.) Tourism

Douglass event: Talbot County (Md.) Tourism

RENAISSANCE FAIRE AT FURNACE TOWN

Late September in Snow Hill, Md.
Region: Lower Eastern Shore of Maryland

Travel back in time by half a millennium to celebrate a period of European life remembered for exciting ideas and new ways of thinking. There will be knights and damsels aplenty, some of them belonging to the local chapter of an international group called the Society for Creative Anachronism. They're dedicated to a proposition that's close to my heart—history is fun! Their approach to that involves elaborate costumes and over-the-top play-acting.

Held on the grounds of the Furnace Town Historic Site along the backroads of Worcester County, the event will feature shining armor, powerful queens, period musicians, and lots of craftspeople—from broom makers to blacksmiths to woodworkers and more. For kids (and kids at heart), there will be games, hair braiding, face painting, henna artists, and the like. In one recent year, they even brought in a marching bagpipe band.

Tourism info: Worcester County (Md.) Tourism

BERLIN FIDDLER'S CONVENTION

Late September in Berlin, Md.
Region: Lower Eastern Shore of Maryland

Banjos and fiddles take over the streets in downtown Berlin during this toe-tapping weekend of concerts, competitions, and old-fashioned fun. The "convention" started in the early 1990s as a humble one-afternoon affair, but now stretches across three days and nights, drawing big crowds of bluegrass players and fans from all over the Mid- Atlantic region. In addition to traditional concerts by top-of-the-line regional and national acts, you'll be able to watch talented-but-undiscovered pickers and players from near and far show off their best tunes during competitions in fiddle, banjo, guitar, and band categories. The winners get to head back home with hefty cash prizes in hand.

A small-town atmosphere prevails, with even big-star names on the bill mixing and mingling freely with fans and fellow musicians. Fun jam sessions abound. Food trucks aplenty on the streets. The stages are set up in the midst of a downtown Main Street that ranks among the prettiest on Delmarva. If you've seen the Hollywood megabit "Runaway Bride," you already know that—the film was shot here in Berlin.

TIP JAR: You don't have to just be a spectator. If you or someone you know plays a little bluegrass, get some time in the spotlight by registering in one or another of the performance categories, most of which have youth and adult divisions.

Tourism info: Berlin Chamber of Commerce and/or Worcester County (Md.) Tourism

EIGHT FALL OYSTER FESTIVALS
Various locations in October and November

In other parts of the world, the first chilly nights of autumn bring an end to the outdoor festival season. But when cold winds start blowing here on Delmarva, it's time to break out an extra layer and head out to slurp down bivalves and beer. There are dozens of oyster festivals between October and March. Here are a few fall options.

Chincoteague Oyster Festival

Early October in Chincoteague, Va.

Region: Eastern Shore of Virginia

Usually held on the first Saturday of the month, this one tends to sell out early, so don't procrastinate.

Tourism info: Eastern Shore of Virginia Tourism

Snow Hill Seafood Festival

Mid-October in Snow Hill, Md.

Region: Lower Eastern Shore of Maryland

This all-you-can-eat affair features oysters fixed every which way, plus lots of other seafood treats. Live music, "bottomless" beer, and more.

Tourism info: Worcester County (Md.) Tourism

Mount Harmon Bull & Oyster Roast

Mid-October to Early November in Earleville, Md.

Region: Upper Eastern Shore of Maryland

This one is held under a big tent on a gorgeous old plantation. The manor house should be open for tours. The date in recent years has fluctuated some inside of the wide window here.

Tourism info: Cecil County (Md.) Tourism

Rock Hall Fall Fest

Early/Middle October in Rock Hall, Md.

Region: Upper Eastern Shore of Maryland

This street festival has music, crafts, vendors, and lots and lots of oysters–shucked, fried, stewed, etc.

Tourism info: Kent County (Md.) Tourism

Soule Arnold Oyster Roast

Middle/Late October in Exmore, Va.

Region: Eastern Shore of Virginia

This sweet bit of small-town bliss is held outdoors in a park along Exmore's Main Street.

Tourism info: Eastern Shore of Virginia Tourism

Chesapeake Bay Maritime Museum Oyster Festival

Late October in St. Michaels, Md.

Region: Upper Eastern Shore of Maryland

The museum's annual bivalve bash will have boat rides, live music, and activities geared to all ages.

Tourism info: Talbot County (Md.) Tourism

The Saxis Island Oyster Roast

Early November in Saxis, Va.

Region: Eastern Shore of Virginia

The main event here is an all-you-can-eat BYOB affair in a remote, real-deal watermen town. There will probably be quite an after-party at a nearby tiki bar, Capt. E's Hurricane Grill. I've always had a hard time finding online info about this party, which is why there's a phone number below.

Tourism info: Town of Saxis, Va. (757-824-4792) and/or Eastern Shore of Virginia Tourism and/or Saxis Island Museum

The Brew and Oyster Brawl

Early/Middle November in Easton, Md.
Region: Upper Eastern Shore of Maryland
This one happens at the Tidewater Inn smack dab in the middle of the big town-wide Waterfowl Festival.

Tourism info: Talbot County (Md.) Tourism

Reminder: The best way to keep track of these oyster events and others throughout the year is by subscribing to Month of Fundays, the Secrets of the Eastern Shore newsletter. You can do that at secretsoftheeasternshore.com.

NORTHAMPTON AGRICULTURAL FAIR

Early October in Machipongo, Va.
Region: Eastern Shore of Virginia

Though it's a relative newcomer to the event calendar on the Eastern Shore of Virginia, the Northampton Agricultural Fair can lay claim to deep roots. The agriculture-oriented Keller Fair started back in 1878 and grew into an enormously popular celebration of local culture. The African-American community had a pair of famous fairs back in the day as well, one in Tasley and another in Weirwood.

Alas, these old celebrations faded into the mists of history, but this fair aims to serve as their modern-day incarnation. The grounds of an old middle school in Machipongo will be filled with old tractors and other farm equipment from days gone by. A rumbling parade of those vehicles will be on the schedule, as will an array of tractor races.

Culinary traditions will be front and center, thanks to food vendors serving up local specialties and cooking contests in categories that range from pecan and pumpkin pie to sweet potato pie and sweet potato biscuits. If you're brave enough, you can step into the spotlight during the country-flavored fun here. As of this writing, the reigning skillet-toss champions hit distances of 66 feet, 5 inches (men) and 37 feet, 5 inches (women). If you prefer sit-down contests, snag a spot at the pie-eating table.

Local seafood and oyster aquaculture operations have been on hand in recent years to show off their work. Admission to the festival has been free so far, with a small fee for all-access passes to a bevy of kids activities— hayrides, pumpkin painting, corn boxes, face painting, a petting zoo, and more.

Tourism info: Northampton County Chamber of Commerce and/or Eastern Shore of Virginia Tourism

River Towns Fall Festival

Early October in New Castle and Delaware City, Del.
Region: Upper Delaware

Myriad cycling events in the Delmarva region are geared toward the endurance crowd. The Seagull Century draws some 6,000 riders onto the backroads of Maryland's Lower Eastern Shore every October. In Virginia, the Between the Waters Bike Tour that same month sells out its 1,000 spots many weeks in advance of race day.

With due respect to long-distance bike racers in the audience here, feats on the order of 100-mile "century" rides are not the focus of this book. But the River Towns Ride & Festival is a different breed. A scant 10 miles along flat and pretty Route 9 separate the historic towns of New Castle and Delaware City, the latter of which will be throwing an after-ride party in the waterfront Battery Park with live music, vendors, craft beers, and more.

Both towns are also full of interesting things to see, including some sweet old architecture and gorgeous stretches of Delaware River shoreline. Plus, riding is not really required: You could opt for a seat on a shuttle bus instead.

TIP JAR: In recent years, organizers have offered optional and duplicate extra cycling legs to please those endurance-pedaling fans. One route covers 12 extra miles and leads to the DuPont Environmental Education Center in a third town, Wilmington. Make a double round-trip to all three sites of 64 miles, and you will earn an extra-special gold medal. Me? I'll be at the after-party.

Tourism info: New Castle County (Del.) Tourism

APPLE SCRAPPLE FESTIVAL

Mid-October in Bridgeville, Del.
Region: Lower Delaware

Little towns all over this land look for ways to celebrate their unique heritage and charms, but not many come up with ideas as close to pure genius as the one the people of Bridgeville, Del. devised back in the 1990s. The mid-October Apple Scrapple festival celebrates two pillars of the town's economy—agriculture and mystery meat. Bridgeville has been the home of the famous RAPA Scrapple company since back in 1926.

The event was a hit from the get-go—more than 2,000 people showed up in year one. Nowadays, you will find yourself among more than 20,000 revelers who venture into this middle-of-farmland nowhere to enjoy a big car show, browse hundreds of crafts and vendor tents, and take in live music and other performances.

There is lots of wacky fun over two festive days. Local politicians and celebrities face off in a Scrapple Sling. The Skillet Toss is a ladies-only competition. The rules for Scrapple Chunkin include a comforting disclaimer: "No RAPA Scrapple will be harmed during this event." Amateur chefs enter recipe contests devoted to both title attractions. Local children vie for the coveted title of Little Miss Apple Scrapple. Carnival rides and a Friday night street dance are usually on the bill, too.

Stuff will be happening all over town—and beyond. In recent years, the local Kiwanis Club has put on a Home Decorating Contest to test the creativity of locals when it comes to celebrating apples and scrapple in lawn decor. A shuttle service has been offered to take people out to the countryside for Fun on the Farm wagon rides and other activities at Delaware's oldest apple orchard, T.S. Smith & Sons. Local churches, the library, and the Bridgeville Historical Society get in on the act as well.

Tourism info: Southern Delaware Tourism

AMISH PAROCHIAL SCHOOL AUCTION

Mid-October near Dover, Del.
Region: Upper Delaware

You know you're putting on a pretty good yard sale when you draw more than 10,000 bargain hunters from up and down the Eastern Seaboard—and points beyond—to a private farm along Winding Creek Drive in the countryside west of Dover. A few years back, one of the organizers, Eli Yoder, summed it up this way: "If it's not here, it's probably not made."

The Amish community near Dover may not be as well-known as the one up in Lancaster, Pa., but its population exceeds 1,000, and its history goes back more than a century. For the last 30-plus years, they have run this auction to raise funds for their private schools. Once a Saturday-only affair, it now includes a Friday evening bonus event where select auction items go up for sale early.

The sale on Saturday remains the biggest draw, drawing thousands of customers. Things get rolling at 8 a.m., after five full days of work by volunteers setting up thousands of items under huge, white-topped tents. The offerings are organized into categories that include handmade quilts, Longaberger baskets, new and used furniture, antiques, glassware, collectibles, tools, lumber, windows, doors, and cabinets. Lots of farm treasures are available, too: plants, tractors, tools, and horse tack among them. You could even head home as the proud owner of an Amish buggy—and a horse to pull it, too. Food vendors dot the grounds. A sprawling flea market gives the most obsessive of bargain hunters abundant opportunities to scrounge for dirt-cheap treasures.

Credit cards will work for items in the official auction, but cash will be king when it comes to food vendors and flea marketers. Also, the event is held on a working farm with livestock and other animals—don't bring your dog (unless it's a service animal), as this seems to be a recurring source of frustration for visitors and organizers alike.

Tourism info: Kent County (Del.) Tourism

NANTICOKE RIVER JAMBOREE

Mid-October in Vienna, Md.
Region: Lower Eastern Shore of Maryland

Living history will be front and center here, as re-enactors and craftspeople dramatize the lives and demonstrate the skills of Indians, African Americans, and European Americans. Located along little-traveled Indiantown Road near Vienna, Md., Handsell House rises from a sprawling field like a herald from days gone by. The red-brick gem dating to the late 1700s was rescued from near oblivion a couple of decades back by a group of community volunteers.

That group set out to transform the old joint into a place that tells the stories of the Native Americans, European Americans, and African Americans who have made their homes in this area through the centuries. As of this writing, the Nanticoke River Jamboree ranks as the largest living-history event in Dorchester County. You will find craftspeople demonstrating skills from days gone by. Re-enactors will give talks and chat with visitors about the ups, downs, challenges, and joys folks experienced in times gone by.

Visit a replica Chicone Indian village, where local Native

American tribes will be sharing stories and talking about the techniques their ancestors used in constructing longhouses like this. European- and African-American traditions will be on display as well. The interior of Handsell House will be open for tours. A Nature Walk event has been offered in recent years, along with presentations about the lives of enslaved peoples.

TIP JAR: That word *jamboree* might evoke images of dance bands and beer tents, but that's not the focus here. A food truck or two will be on hand, but this event is mostly about the chance to have up-close encounters with the traditions of centuries gone by.

Tourism info: Dorchester County (Md.) Tourism

UPPER SHORE DECOY SHOW

Mid-October in North East, Md.
Region: Upper Eastern Shore of Maryland

Once upon a time, the wooden decoy was a lowly bit of hunting handiwork. Carved for the utilitarian purpose of luring ducks into hunting range, they were stored willy-nilly in old burlap bags during off-seasons. They seemed destined for oblivion when cheap, mass-produced plastic ducks came on the scene in the early years of the 20th century.

But then something strange and wonderful happened. Some decoy carvers responded to that marketing challenge by stepping up their artistic game, creating ducks that were more sculptural and less functional. Today, decoys are regarded as objects of high art that belong not in the bilge of a hunting boat, but in places of prominence in museum cases and pricey private collections.

One of the country's longest-running decoy shows is hosted by the Upper Bay Museum in Cecil County, Md. and features an array of exquisitely crafted birds by nationally known carvers. The event has been held in various locations in recent years. It usually opens on Friday evening with a ticketed preview party followed by a public auction of select decoys to support the museum. The main event is Saturday. In addition to decoy displays, there will be demonstrations, kids activities, vendors, and more.

Tourism info: Cecil County (Md.) Tourism

REHOBOTH BEACH JAZZ FESTIVAL AND TRUE BLUE JAZZ FESTIVAL

Both in mid-October in Rehoboth Beach, Del.
Region: Lower Delaware

One sure sign that the folks who put together the Rehoboth Beach Jazz Festival aren't kidding around: A while back, they trademarked an immodest slogan, "The Greatest Jazz Festival in the World!"—complete with that exclamation point. The festival, which is now more than 30 years old, unfolds in a dizzying array of concerts in at least four different locations—the boardwalk bandstand, the convention center, a local church, and a famous watering hole. The talent lineup is always chock full of big national names.

But those official shows are just the beginning. Just about every joint in town with a performance space books compatible acts, so every evening adds up to a jazz pub crawl that runs from one end of town to the other.

Another musical treat, the True Blue Jazz Festival is usually up and running in this same window. Most of those shows happen at the Boardwalk Plaza Hotel and the local firehouse, with a focus less on modern jazz and more on mainstream classics out of the "Great American Songbook" of the early 20th century.

If and when you need a break from live music—hey, you're in Rehoboth. It's the foodiest of Delmarva's beach resorts. It's got a glorious oceanfront boardwalk. Cape Henlopen State Park is just north of town. Shopping options run the gamut, from quaint downtown boutiques to sprawling outlet malls.

Tourism info: Southern Delaware Tourism

MEET AT THE TABLE

Mid-October in Painter, Va.
Region: Eastern Shore of Virginia

This culinary celebration of harvest time is a thoroughly homegrown affair. Held on a 3.5-acre farm where the oldest in an array of historic buildings dates to the 1690s, Meet at the Table is a showcase for the talents and artistry of locals, from chefs, brewers, and distillers to farmers, watermen, and artists.

The project is the work of Kate Meyer and John Fitzpatrick, the couple behind Chatham Flower Farm. Pretty much everything you'll see while wandering the event site will be grown or created locally. That includes decorations as well as delicacies, as the tables will be awash in the deep autumnal shades of fresh-cut flowers. Live music is part of the deal, along with an array of silent and live auction items. Proceeds will boost a local non-profit.

The menu changes every year, of course, but it always

sounds fabulous. One of the appetizers at a recent Meet at the Table was braised lamb and apple quesadilla on saffron parsnip purée and topped with preserves, lemon, and julienne apple. One of the desserts that same year was persimmon and créme fraîche layered panna cotta with hazelnut shortbread and spent grain tuile. So, to sum up: YUM!

Tourism Info: Eastern Shore of Virginia Tourism

GOOD BEER FESTIVAL

Mid-October in Salisbury, Md.
Region: Lower Eastern Shore of Maryland

The setting here is gorgeous—Pemberton Park covers more than 250 acres on the southwestern outskirts of Salisbury, Md. and features 4.5 miles of hiking paths running through forests, meadows, and marshlands. The Good Beer Festival usually features more than 50 breweries and runs on Friday evening and Saturday afternoon.

In the popular Local Beer Garden, the spotlight is on just that—a dozen or so brewing stars from the Delmarva region. Live music runs continuously, with styles ranging from singer-songwriters to R&B to classic rock. In addition to an array of craft vendors and food tents, you'll get to play beer-themed carnival games and engage in other bouts of silliness.

The event happens on an expansive lawn that stretches out in front of Pemberton Hall, a restored plantation house built in the 1740s. The lawn is bordered on one side with striking "snake" fencing from that period and on another with a little grove of apple trees. The property faces down toward those hiking trails and the Wicomico River, so you will have ample options when you need to take a break from drinking.

Tourism info: Wicomico County (Md.) Tourism

ZOMBIE FEST

Middle/Late October in Milton, Del.
Region: Lower Delaware

The culmination of this over-the-top Halloween extravaganza has a small army of zombies wobbling through downtown Milton after dark in a horrifyingly fun little parade. No worries about that perfect, blemish-free face of yours—just get there early and stop at a makeup station. In one recent year, that was staffed by students from the Delaware Learning Institute of Cosmetology.

There is lots more on tap. The festival grounds in and around the Milton Theatre will likely have old-school circus freak shows, fire-eating daredevils, a bed of nails, and more. A troupe of zombie pirates might show up. The lineup may change from year to year, but you get the idea. There will be costume contests, a "Zombify Your Car" competition, live music, spooky dancing, bounce houses, a "Rocky Horror" showing, and lots more fun.

The fun starts in late afternoon, with the big Zombie Walk stepping off once it's dark enough. As the event slogan goes, "There's nothing better for a community to feel alive than by becoming the 'undead'... together!"

Tourism info: Southern Delaware Tourism

Ocean City Sunfest

Middle/Late October in Ocean City, Md.
Region: Lower Eastern Shore of Maryland

Just as Springfest in May marks an early start to the tourist season in Ocean City, so Sunfest marks its late close. The weather might still be warm enough to dip toes—and perhaps even dive—into the ocean, but that window will be closing by the time you arrive at this long-weekend extravaganza centered on the Inlet parking area near the lower end of the boardwalk. The event used to be in late September, but organizers switched recently to this new October weekend.

Two stages of live music usually run all day long here, and 30 or so food vendors serve up everything from resort junk food to Amish baked goods and ethnic specialties. Scores of vendors will be set up under humongous tents, displaying souvenirs, knickknacks, housewares, one clothing. The biggest draw in those tents will be arts and crafts, as the array of pottery, jewelry, painting, and other works earned Sunfest a spot in one recent ranking of the country's best craft shows.

There should be plenty of activities to keep kids happy and running, including inflatable fun houses and hayrides. The switch to October seems to have added a Halloween focus to things, so expect some spooky fun and games as well. Needless to say, the joys of the boardwalk will be a short stroll (or tram ride) away.

Tourism info: Ocean City (Md.) Tourism and/or Worcester County (Md.) Tourism

SEAWITCH FESTIVAL

Late October in Rehoboth Beach and Dewey Beach, Del.
Region: Lower Delaware

Basically, Halloween on steroids. For a place whose roots lie in the religious "camp meetings" of devout Methodists in the late 1800s, modern-day Rehoboth Beach sure loves paying homage to the most pagan of our holidays. The Seawitch Festival is by far the biggest celebration of Halloween on the Delmarva Peninsula, as it usually encompasses more than a hundred different events that stretch across three days and extend into nearby Dewey Beach.

When the event began in 1990, the notion that tourists might want to visit the beach outside of the traditional summer-time window still ranked as a marketing pipe dream. But when 5,000 people showed up that first year to enjoy a few activities in a dirt-covered parking lot, Seawitch organizers realized there were on to something. Nowadays, the event draws crowds of 150,000 or more

The showstopper is a Saturday morning parade down Rehoboth Avenue filled with giant balloons, marching bands, colorful mummers, and costumed creatures. Recent years have also featured a Haunted Bonfire Beach Party and Creepy Grave Yard Trail in Dewey Beach. A third highlight is for the little ones in your life: Along the Children's Fantasy Trail at Cape Henlopen State Park, trick-or-treaters will meet characters from their favorite storybooks. Vendor tents abound, along with arts activities and fun games. Think pony rides, contests, live music, history talks, spooky movies, crafts demonstrations—the event program here has been known to run to more than 50 pages.

Some skills to practice in advance: Broom tossing, pumpkin-seed-spitting, and slime-making. They have ranked in recent years among the myriad contests on the Seawitch bill.

Tourism info: Southern Delaware Tourism

SULTANA DOWNRIGGING FESTIVAL

Late October/Early November in Chestertown, Md.
Region: Upper Eastern Shore of Maryland

Experience the romance and adventure of the Age of Sail at one of the largest annual gatherings of replica tall ships on the Eastern Seaboard. There will be bluegrass bands playing and experts talking during this weekend. Local distilleries and wineries will be pouring. Fireworks will explode on the Chester River waterfront over a forest of ship masts.

But those are not the biggest draws. People come to Downrigging from all over for a chance to get up close and personal with the tall ships of days gone by as they sail on the Chester River. Started back in the late 1990s, Downrigging quickly grew into one of the region's biggest maritime-heritage events.

At least half a dozen replica schooners and other big vessels will likely be in attendance, along with a good number of skipjacks, tugs, and other smaller wooden boats of historical interest. You'll be able to see all the vessels up close, dockside. You can also climb aboard the biggest ones as they set out for public sails, but it's best to sign up for those weeks in advance (maybe even a couple months, actually) as they sell out quickly.

Each ship has its own stories to tell about American history, and crew members share those stories with passengers while underway. You can clamber below decks and feel the rolling of waves underfoot. Those crew members might even invite you to help hoist a sail or two.

Tourism info: Kent County (Md.) Tourism

EASTON WATERFOWL FESTIVAL

Early November in Easton, Md.
Region: Upper Eastern Shore of Maryland

Back in 1971 the Waterfowl Festival began with three small and sparsely attended art exhibits. Even then, however, organizers were predicting that the festival would "grow into something extraordinary." They were right, of course—the event now sprawls across a slew of venues all over town and draws tens of thousands of visitors.

Things usually kick off with opening ceremonies and a ticketed preview party on Thursday evening. The three jam-packed days that follow will have you wandering here, there, and everywhere in Easton's downtown (and beyond) to enjoy fly-fishing sessions, dock-dog acrobatics, retriever displays, short films, duck- and goose-calling competitions, live-raptor shows—the list goes on and on.

Art exhibits are still a big part of the festival, with 75 or so "featured" artists and another 75 or so vendors showing sculptures, paintings, photos, sculptures, and more. For kids, there will be things like waterfowl-calling lessons, a fishing derby, and storytelling sessions.

Most folks will want to buy a pass to get into those "official" festival events, but there is also a free street party aspect to Waterfowl weekend. Many food tents, live-music performances, wine-tasting pavilions, and beer gardens will be open to non-pass holders. Plus, lots of restaurants and cultural groups schedule their own special events (some free, some ticketed) outside of the official festival. The Tidewater Inn, for instance, throws its Brew & Oyster Brawl bash on Saturday.

TIP JAR: The nearby town of Oxford usually has its Antique Show & Sale this same weekend—that event goes back fiftysome years.

Tourism info: Talbot County (Md.) Tourism

18TH CENTURY MARKET FAIR

Early November in Dover, Del.
Region: Upper Delaware

The Dover Green is a staid affair today, full of stately buildings and cultural attractions befitting a state capitol. But back before the Revolutionary War, this same turf hosted raucous market fairs where tradespeople and traveling merchants hawked goods in an atmosphere filled with musicians, acrobats, and other performers.

The First State Heritage Park brings those wild and wooly days back to life on a Saturday in early November. In addition to period dance and music, you might get to watch a "conjurer" turn magic tricks, an "equilibrist" walk the tightrope, and a traveling "medicine show" serving concoctions guaranteed to cure whatever ails you.

Visit stalls and shops where you can watch blacksmiths, potters, brewmasters, woodworkers, tavern cooks, and soap makers tackle their crafts. The kids will be able to learn about (and play) 18th-century games. Several historic attractions within walking distance here are part of the First State Heritage Park,

129

including the John Bell House, the Old State House, the Biggs Museum of American Art, and the Johnson Victrola Museum—they're all definitely worth a visit.

Tourism info: Kent County (Del.) Tourism

RETURN DAY

The days after November elections in Georgetown, Del.
Region: Lower Delaware

Technically, this isn't an annual event—it only happens every two years when there are big election dates in November. But Return Day dates back to 1792, so hey, let's cut the event some slack. Back in those days state law required voters in Sussex County to travel to the county seat of Georgetown to cast their votes. Everyone would "return" two days later to hear the official announcement of winners and losers. The alcohol flowed freely on "Return Day," and the gathering eventually morphed into one of the most fun and interesting civic electoral traditions in the whole country.

There will be some festivities on Wednesday evening, with the main events unfolding on Thursday. The ox-roast tradition was launched way back when by Democrats. The parade was a Republican innovation. Traditionally, each race gets its own horse-drawn carriage, with the winner facing forward during the parade while the loser faces backward. After the parade comes a literal "burying of the hatchet," with the axe of political division getting buried in a box of sand imported for the occasion from nearby Lewes. There will be music, there will be town criers, there will be guys in top hats and ladies in old-time dresses.

Tourism info: Georgetown, Del. And/or Southern Delaware Tourism

FIVE HOLIDAY LIGHT SHOWS & DECOR DISPLAYS

Mid-November through December
Various locations

Brighten up your holiday season by gathering up family and friends for an expedition to one or more of Delmarva's biggest displays of holiday lights and seasonal décor.

Winter Wonderfest in Milton, Del.
Region: Lower Delaware
Take a leisurely 1.5-mile ride through the elaborate light displays set up through the Hudson Fields site and then enjoy hayrides, ice skating, carnival rides, and Santa's Workshop.
Tourism info: Southern Delaware Tourism

Winterfest of Lights in Ocean City, Md.
Region: Lower Eastern Shore of Maryland
More than 1 million bulbs go into the displays at 58-acre Northside Park. Afterward, enjoy hot chocolate in a heated pavilion and get photos taken with a certain jolly man. Kids can hop on a Winterfest Express mini-train that rides past fairy-tale-themed exhibits.
Tourism info: Ocean City (Md.) Tourism and/or Worcester County (Md.) Tourism

Longwood Christmas in Kennett Square, Pa.

Region: Upper Delaware (and then some)

At Longwood Gardens north of Wilmington, Del. (just across the Pennsylvania line, actually), you will wander a humongous glass-walled conservatory awash in elegant décor, stroll paths lined with towering trees filled with colorful bulbs, and visit gardens adorned with glowing orbs. Fire pits, caroling, and hot chocolate, too.

Info: Longwood Gardens

Yuletide at Winterthur in Wilmington, Del.

Region: Upper Delaware

This 175-room mansion from the early 1900s will have a spectacular display of Christmas trees and a dollhouse "mansion" sprawling across 18 rooms and 1,000 miniature figures. Live, one-man shows of "A Christmas Carol" are usually on the bill, too.

Tourism Info: Wilmington (Del.) Tourism

The Holidays at Hagley in Wilmington, Del.

Region: Upper Delaware

This 1803 du Pont mansion honors that famous family's European roots during the holiday season by exploring Christmas traditions in France. You'll also be able to stroll through centuries of American holiday décor. On weekends, there might be family-

oriented cookie-decorating and ornament-making sessions, too.
Tourism Info: Wilmington (Del.) Tourism

Two Open Studio Tours

Artisans Guild Studio Tour in Virginia
Late November on the Eastern Shore of Virginia

The Southeastern Delaware Artists Studio Tour
Mid-November in Southern Delaware

The backroads are always out there waiting, but too often they end up the subject of empty promises we make to ourselves: "The next time I come up Route 13, I'm going to leave extra time to wander around."

You can finally fulfill that promise by joining in the Artisans Guild Studio Tour that's put on by the Eastern Shore of Virginia Artisans Guild on the Friday and Saturday after Thanksgiving. Nearly 50 artists display works at 15 to 20 stops that run from down in Cape Charles to up in Onancock. Along the way, you'll be following a map that leads through the off-the-highway likes of Belle Haven, Pungoteague, and Wachapreague.

The works you'll see will run the gamut from painting and sculpture to jewelry, fiber, ceramics, glassware, and stonework. The tour has included wild-card stops in recent years, too—a vineyard and a flower farm among them. Some historic stops will likely be on the agenda as well.

133

More artsy fun happens on this same weekend up in Chincoteague, where the annual Holly Day Market serves up a mix of old-school decoy carvings, antiques, and modern-day wildlife art. Expect to find 75 or so vendors in the two buildings where the Chincoteague Cultural Alliance puts on this show.

If Southern Delaware is a more convenient destination for you, the Southeastern Delaware Artists Studio Tour is a similar event on the mid-November calendar. In one recent year, the tour featured stops at 13 studios and six galleries, with locations spread out among Rehoboth Beach, Bethany Beach, Ocean View, Dagsboro, Clarksville, and more.

Tourism info (Virginia event): Eastern Shore of Virginia Tourism. Tourism info (Delaware event): Southern Delaware Tourism

WATERFOWL WEEKEND

Late November in Chincoteague, Va.
Region: Eastern Shore of Virginia

Think of this as a great way to ditch that dazed, bloated feeling that follows Thanksgiving overindulgence. Every year on that holiday weekend, the 14,000-acre Chincoteague National Wildlife Refuge gives a gift to nature lovers, opening up a seven-mile-long Service Road that is otherwise off-limits. Be sure to arrive in time for the early afternoon window when you can pull onto that northbound route and follow it past Shoveler Pool, Mallard Pool, and Sow Pond. You'll also have extended hours of vehicle access to the three-mile-long Wildlife Loop Trail. If you're feeling ambitious, you could choose to pedal or hike your way along one or both of those routes.

If you've never been to the refuge before, stop at Bateman Center to get your bearings and pick up a map. There will be exhibits to see and videos to watch. Staffers will be on hand to help you plan out your itinerary. The most famous trail at the refuge leads to the base of the red-and-white striped Assateague lighthouse, which was built shortly after the Civil War. My favorite walk starts along the Woodland Trail and then veers onto the Bivalve Trail on the way out to the shores of Tom's Cove.

If the weather cooperates, head to the beach here and take a southbound stroll to "Fisherman's Hook," where you can keep your eye out for the ruins of an old fish factory and the site of an old Coast Guard station.

Tourism info: Chincoteague Chamber of Commerce and/or Eastern Shore of Virginia Tourism

Shore Bets!

CHAPTER FOUR:
WINTER EVENTS

12 Days of Christmas, Plus Two

December on Delmarva could be a book unto itself, with all the holiday parades, concerts, tree lightings, block parties, and theatrical events that unfold as towns and civic groups celebrate the Christmas season.

I usually work up a guide to 100-plus holiday events for the Secrets of the Eastern Shore website and newsletter, so look there as the season approaches for a fuller range of choices.

Sign up for the newsletter on the website: SecretsoftheEasternShore.com. Or send me a note and I'll sign you up manually: SecretsoftheEasternShore@gmail.com

In the meantime, here are a dozen Delmarva holiday classics:

Festive Fridays

The day after Thanksgiving through Christmas in Cape Charles, Va.

Region: Eastern Shore of Virginia

In downtown Cape Charles on Friday evenings during the season, there will likely be carriage rides, a Santa House, holiday movies, late shopping, and more.

Tourism info: Eastern Shore of Virginia Tourism and/or Cape Charles Tourism

Wilmington & Western Railroad Holiday Rides

Thanksgiving through Christmas in Wilmington, Del.
Region: Upper Delaware
This old railroad line is all about nostalgic, steam-powered joy-rides. Sign up for one or both of the holiday-themed excursions—a daytime Santa Claus Express and a nighttime Holiday Lights Express.

Tourism info: Wilmington (Del.) Tourism

The Rescue Fire Company Christmas Train Garden

Throughout December in Cambridge, Md.
Region: Lower Eastern Shore of Maryland
You'll have a slew of holiday train displays to choose from during the holidays, but this is probably the granddaddy of the bunch, up and running in the old firehouse in the heart of downtown Cambridge since the mid-1930s. Visit the nearby Crab Basket Christmas Tree while you're there.

Tourism info: Dorchester County (Md.) Tourism

Schellville Enchanted Winter Celebration

Thanksgiving through Christmas in Rehoboth Beach, Del.
Region: Lower Delaware
Set up on the highway in Rehoboth Beach, this relative newbie of a tradition has had miniature Christmas house displays, Santa vis-

its, ice skating, a beer garden, local artists, and lots more. Bonus: It might be snowing at Schellville, no matter what the weatherman says.

Tourism info: Southern Delaware Tourism

Christmas in Odessa

Early December in Odessa, Del.
Region: Upper Delaware
One of Delmarva's oldest holiday house tours, this self-guided affair has more than 20 stops within a few strolling-friendly blocks. Music, Santa, holiday greens, a food truck, etc.

Tourism info: New Castle County (Del.) Tourism

Dickens of a Christmas Weekend

Early December in Chestertown, Md.
Region: Upper Eastern Shore of Maryland
This Victorian-themed three-day weekend in downtown Chestertown is filled with bonfires, street performers, kids' activities, "London Row" shopping stalls, and more. Costumes encouraged!

Tourism info: Kent County (Md.) Tourism

Holiday Joy Christmas Concert

Early December in multiple locations
The Mid-Atlantic Symphony Orchestra spreads "Holiday Joy" in annual Christmas shows—usually, there's one in Easton, Md.; one in Lewes, Del.; and one in Ocean City, Md.

Info: Mid-Atlantic Symphony

Milton Holly Festival

Early December in Milton, Del.

Region: Lower Delaware

Southern Delaware used to be so famous for its hand-crafted wreaths that it was known as the "Land of Holly." That turn of history is behind this civic gathering with food, house tours, vendors, and more.

Info: Southern Delaware Tourism

Brownsville Holiday Open House

Early December in Nassawadox, Va.

Region: Eastern Shore of Virginia

Enjoy wagon rides, campfires, cider, and more on the grounds of a history-laden farm that is now the 1,200-acre Brownsville Preserve, owned by the Nature Conservancy.

Tourism info: Eastern Shore of Virginia Tourism

Holiday Open House at Rockwood Park

Early December in Wilmington, Del.

Region: Upper Delaware

In addition to traditional Santa visits and festive crafts, you'll probably see performances by local dance troupes that run the gamut from ballet and jazz to Mexican folk and line-dancing Bollywood.

Tourism info: Wilmington (Del.) Tourism

Caroling on the Circle
Mid-December in Georgetown, Del.
Region: Lower Delaware
Gather in a sweet patch of traffic-circle greenery surrounded by historic buildings in the seat of Sussex County to sing carols. Hot chocolate and cookies afterward at the local firehouse. Bring along non-perishable food items—a food drive is part of the deal.
Tourism info: Southern Delaware Tourism

Christmas in St. Michaels
Mid-December in St. Michaels, Md.
Region: Upper Eastern Shore of Maryland
In addition to a fabulous Saturday morning parade, this weekend-long celebration usually features a tour of homes, gingerbread houses, music, church meals with a holiday flair, and more.
Tourism info: Talbot County (Md.) Tourism

Wreaths Across America
Mid-December in various locations
Donors and volunteers team up to make sure seasonal wreaths are placed on the graves of veterans in cemeteries around the country. In recent years, eightish Delmarva cemeteries have participated. You can support the effort either by making a donation or by signing on in advance as a wreath-laying volunteer.
Info: Wreaths Across America

Christmas in Onancock

Mid-December in Onancock, Va.
Region: Eastern Shore of Virginia
This three-day weekend on Onancock Creek usually includes luminaria-lined streets and downtown festivities on Friday evening, a tour of homes and a music festival on Saturday, and a Christmas parade on Sunday. Somewhere in there, Santa will arrive by boat to join the party.
      Tourism info: Onancock Business & Civic Association and/or Eastern Shore of Virginia Tourism

9 NEW YEAR'S EVE PARTIES AND DROPS

Various locations on Dec. 31
Ring in the new year, Delmarva style. Here are nine of the region's most popular New Year's Eve traditions.

New Year's Eve: Berlin Ball Drop

Location: Berlin, Md.
Region: Lower Eastern Shore of Maryland
A special kids-oriented ball drop happens early on. A street party with food trucks, music, and libations leads up to the traditional Ball Drop at midnight.
      Tourism info: Berlin Chamber of Commerce and/or Worcester County (Md.) Tourism

New Year's Eve: Cape Charles Crab Pot Drop

Location: Cape Charles, Va.

Region: Eastern Shore of Virginia

The Crab Pot Drop usually happens along Mason Avenue, with live music and other festive activities starting around 9pm.

Tourism info: Eastern Shore of Virginia Tourism

New Year's Eve: Chincoteague Horseshoe Drop

Location: Chincoteague, Va.

Region: Eastern Shore of Virginia

The Horseshoe Drop honors the famed Chincoteague ponies, of course. There is a fun costume contest and promenade as well, with a different dress-up theme set for each new year.

Tourism info: Chincoteague Chamber of Commerce and/ or Eastern Shore of Virginia Tourism

New Year's Eve: The Crisfield Oyster Drop

Location: Crisfield, Md.

Region: Lower Eastern Shore of Maryland

The bivalve drop here happens outside at midnight, but some of the festivities leading up to it are held in the heated confines of the local library.

Tourism info: Somerset County (Md.) Tourism

New Year's Eve: First Night Talbot (with Crab Drop)

Location: Easton, Md.

Region: Upper Eastern Shore of Maryland

You might want to take in both Crab Drops here, as the one for early-to-bed types usually happens in concert with a fun Parade of Sea Creatures. The other one happens at midnight. Fun, alcohol-free events all around town as part of the First Night Talbot festivities.

Tourism info: Talbot County (Md.) Tourism

New Year's Eve: Lewes Anchor Drop

Location: Lewes, Del.

Region: Lower Delaware

Head to Canalfront Park to watch an anchor drop down the mast of the historic Lightship Overfalls come midnight. Music, bonfire, hot chocolate, too.

Tourism info: Southern Delaware Tourism

New Year's Eve: Ocean City Fireworks

Location: Ocean City, Md.

Region: Lower Eastern Shore of Maryland

The big show is at Northside Park come midnight. You can enjoy the famous Winterfest of Lights display in the hours leading up to the big bangs.

Tourism info: Ocean City (Md.) Tourism and/or Worcester County (Md.) Tourism

New Year's Eve: Princess Anne Muskrat Drop

Location: Princess Anne, Md.
Region: Lower Eastern Shore of Maryland
The slogan here says it all: "Free. Weird. Fun." Enjoy music, dancing, games, and food in the streets as part of the buildup to the big "Midnight Muskrat Dive," starring a rodent named Marshall.
Tourism info: Somerset County (Md.) Tourism

New Year's Eve: Salisbury Ball Drop

Location: Salisbury, Md.
Region: Lower Eastern Shore of Maryland
The streets of downtown will be filled with live music, beer, wine, and food trucks in the run-up to this traditional Ball Drop.
Tourism info: Downtown Salisbury (Md.) and/or Wicomico County (Md.) Tourism

NEW YEAR'S DAY PLUNGES AND HIKES

Various locations on Jan. 1
First, the plunges: Thousands of brave souls on Delmarva start the year with a mid-winter dip into ocean or bay. Some make a spectacle of themselves at these charity events, with silly hats and ridiculous bathing garb. Others keep a low profile, taking the briefest of plunges before hightailing it over to the hot chocolate line.

New Year's Day Penguin Swim
Location: Ocean City, Md.
Tourism info: Ocean City (Md.) Tourism and/or Worcester County (Md.) Tourism

New Year's Day Dewey Dunk
Location: Dewey Beach, Del.
Tourism info: Southern Delaware Tourism and/or Dewey Business Partnership

New Year's Day Exercise Like the Eskimos
Location: Bethany Beach, Del.
Tourism info: Southern Delaware Tourism

New Year's Day Polar Pony Plunge
Location: Chincoteague, Va.
Tourism info: Chincoteague Chamber of Commerce and/or Eastern Shore of Virginia Tourism

First Day in the Bay
Location: Cape Charles, Va.
Tourism info: Eastern Shore of Virginia Tourism and/or Cape Charles Citizens for Central Park

Next, the strolls: If that midwinter plunging seems insane to you, no worries. Choose instead to bundle up and welcome the year by joining in a group nature walk instead. A bunch of state parks on the peninsula hold First Day Hikes in the great outdoors.

First Day Hikes in Delaware State Parks
Various locations
When I go looking for these every year, I search this phrase: "First day hikes in Delaware State Parks." It's worked so far!

First Day Hikes in Maryland State Parks
Various locations
Same thing here: Search for the phrase "First day hikes in Maryland State Parks."

P.S.: That search will get statewide results. Here is an alphabetical list of the Eastern Shore parks: Assateague, Bohemia River, Cypress Branch, Elk Neck, Fair Hill NRMA, Harriet Tubman Underground Railroad, Janes Island, Martinak, Pocomoke River, Tuckahoe, and Wye Island NRMA.

First Day Hike at Kiptopeke State Park
Location: Near Cape Charles, Va.
In Virginia, a hike has been held in recent years at Kiptopeke State Park near Cape Charles. That should be on the park's site. If there are other Virginia hikes, you might be able to find them through Eastern Shore of Virginia Tourism.

WINTER WONDERS AT LONGWOOD GARDENS

January/February in Kennett Square, Pa.
Region: Upper Delaware (and then some)

There are two wintertime reasons to take the winding roads through the hills north of Wilmington and cross the border into Pennsylvania to find your way to the 1,000-acre Longwood Gardens. The first is to remind yourself by way of this gloriously designed landscape just how much beauty winter offers, even if that beauty isn't as colorful as what nature serves up in other seasons.

The second is that Longwood's conservatory ranks among the largest such structures in the world, which means that it can deliver generous doses of natural color and life in a season when those things are in short supply.

One big draw here is orchids, and if you find *Orchidaceae* fascinating, you're in good company. The ancient Greeks regarded these delicate flowers as symbols of love and sex. The Aztecs mixed orchids into a drink that boosted their reserves of power and strength. In China, the orchid has long served as a Confucian symbol of friendship and integrity. In the past, Longwood's expert designers have served up floating orchids, climbing orchids, "canopies" of orchids, "passageways" of orchids, "meadows" of orchids, and "waterfalls" of orchids.

There will be more to explore, too: Parts of the Peirce-du Pont house date to the 1730s. Check the Longwood calendar if you want to time your adventure so as to take a tour led by an expert or connect a young companion with a hands-on educational session.

Info: Longwood Gardens

WINTER DELMARVA BIRDING WEEKEND

Late January in various locations
Region: Lower Eastern Shore of Maryland and Southern Delaware

The trips offered during this birding bonanza will be led by experts who love sharing their favorite hideaways, ponds, and trails in Southern Delaware and the Lower Eastern Shore of Maryland. You'll join them in search of avian bliss aboard boats, along hiking trails, and in car caravans. Your fellow adventurers will run the gamut from beginner to expert—it's a great way to meet new and interesting folks.

In recent years, the agenda has included trips to Assateague Island, the shoreline of Chincoteague Bay, Bombay Hook National Wildlife Refuge, the James Farm Ecological Preserve, Burton's Island, and Cape Henlopen State Park. A cruise out on Delaware Bay has been in the mix as well. Each day ends with birding camaraderie by way of a "Tally Rally" review of the day's sightings in a local eatery or watering hole. Such visits to homegrown businesses are a key part of the mission—Delmarva Birding wants to spread the word that environmentally friendly tourism can help give small-town economies a boost.

The trip menu here is a la carte, so you can sign up for the whole weekend if you want, or you can choose one or two jaunts on a single day. If warm-weather birding is more your style, search for the Delmarva Birding website to check out lots of other trips they offer during the course of the year.

Tourism info: Worcester County (Md.) Tourism and Southern Delaware Tourism

THREE FIRE & ICE FESTIVALS

Quiet Resorts Fire & Ice Festival
Late January or early February in Bethany Beach, Ocean View, and Millville, Del.
Region: Lower Delaware
Tourism info: Southern Delaware Tourism

The Cambridge Ice & Oyster Festival
January or February in Cambridge, Md.
Region: Lower Eastern Shore of Maryland
Tourism info: Dorchester County (Md.) Tourism

Chesapeake Fire & Ice Festival
Mid-February in Easton, Md.
Region: Upper Eastern Shore of Maryland
Tourism info: Talbot County (Md.) Tourism

Chainsaws, chisels, and beams of light are the tools of the artistic trade on display at these three relative newcomers to the winter calendar. The Delaware event here began as a Bethany Beach-only affair, but has now grown to include nearby towns. You'll find at least one big signature piece in each burg, as well as smaller, more intricate works set up along main downtown streets. You might want to make sure you're in Bethany Beach when it comes time for the oceanfront bonfire and s'mores party. The focus here is on nighttime viewing, with evocative lighting built into every display. Other highlights include a live sculpting demo and a closing "Smash Party" on Sunday, during which the artworks explode into cubes and shards.

Folks on the western end of the peninsula have had two Fire & Ice parties to choose from in recent years. The event in Easton debuted in 2020, with festivities getting underway at a Friday night Ice Block Party with street music and other entertainment, along with a live sculpture demo. Works were on display all day long here, not just at nighttime, and the festival had related events at the Talbot County Library and in an indoor family fun center with carnival-style games. This affair, too, closed with a destructive flair, during a Sunday Ice Breaker Party.

Despite a heavy snowfall, the Cambridge event was a big success on its first time around in 2022. The sculptures were mostly gathered together here, on an event site tucked behind the downtown business district in a small pocket park and an adjacent parking lot. The work was first rate, as were the oysters and the libations. One highlight: An ice bench where you could take a seat next to Harriet Tubman of Underground Railroad fame.

DEATH BY CHOCOLATE

Mid-February in Chincoteague, Va.
Region: Eastern Shore of Virginia

As autopsy results go, maybe this doesn't sound so bad? The Historic Main Street Merchants of Chincoteague sweeten the pot for your Valentine's excursion on the Friday and Saturday of a weekend close to Feb. 14. All you lovebirds have to do is pick up a playing card, then stroll from place to place in the downtown, enjoying a different chocolate treat and some fun socializing at each stop.

Be warned, though: While Death by Chocolate is sweet, it's also an endurance test. The fact that there are more than 20 stops involved inspires some folks to split the tour between Friday evening and Saturday afternoon. Get your card stamped along the way. At the closing party on Saturday—yes, still more chocolate will be served!—organizers will use those cards to draw winning tickets for prizes donated by participating businesses.

Tourism info: Chincoteague Chamber of Commerce and/or Eastern Shore of Virginia Tourism

THE SEASIDE BOAT SHOW

Mid-February in Ocean City, Md.
Region: Lower Eastern Shore of Maryland

Most boaters endure dreadful bouts of withdrawal as winter drags on. The vessels they love have been up on blocks for months. They can't tinker with engines or fiddle with gear. Good lord, they have to wear socks every day—when will the nightmare end?

Think of a trip to the Seaside Boat Show as a salve for that cabin fever. During three days at the convention center in Ocean City, you'll be able to ogle 350-plus boats from 50 or so dealers. Nearly 150 exhibitors will be showing off the latest in fishing and boating gizmos.

You'll do just fine when the sun goes down, as a decent number of Ocean City restaurants and bars remain open on winter weekends. With a little luck on the weather front, you might even get to take a sun-kissed stroll on the beach to help fill your mind with visions of springtime cruises ahead.

Tourism info: Ocean City (Md.) Tourism and/or Worcester County (Md.) Tourism

BARRIER ISLANDS CENTER OYSTER ROAST

Late February in Machipongo, Va.
Region: Eastern Shore of Virginia

You may have no choice but to endure the winter season, but you do have choices when it comes to how to endure it. Think of the Barrier Islands Center Oyster Roast as a late-winter opportunity to send the season out in style.

Bundle up, as you'll spend much of the night outside under a tent. No real worries, though—if necessary, you should be able to sidle up to one of the big heaters that will be up and running. Traditionally, it's experts at local oyster houses who handle the roasting of wild seaside oysters and the steaming of clams. There will be plenty of other items on the menu, too—some BBQ, perhaps, and some soup, that kind of thing.

There will be libations and music, of course. And there will be fun auction items as proceeds here support the museum, which does a great job preserving and cherishing the history of those barrier islands.

Fair warning: Year in and year out, this event sells out in the blink of an eye. Tickets usually go on sale to museum members first. What's left—and it probably won't be too many tickets—then becomes available to the public. If you want to go, get a membership first or, at a minimum, start paying attention as soon as the New Year rolls around.

Tourism info: Eastern Shore of Virginia Tourism

THE OUTDOOR SHOW AND THE WORLD CHAMPIONSHIP OF MUSKRAT SKINNING

Late February in Golden Hill, Md.
Region: Lower Eastern Shore of Maryland

I saved the best two for last. Who will be crowned as world champion muskrat skinners this year? You can find out by venturing down into the vast marshland of South Dorchester County, where the old ways of trappers, hunters, and watermen still run strong. This legendary event—it was featured in a PBS special called "Muskrat Lovely" a few years back—is a Friday/Saturday celebration of those traditions held in an elementary school in the middle of marshland nowhere.

You'll sit on bleachers in the school gym while cheering on the men, women, and young people competing for the title of world champion muskrat skinner in various categories. You'll see which local teen gets crowned "Miss Outdoors" in a talent contest full of old-school charm. Watch duck-calling competitions. See hunting dogs strut their stuff. Wander through the displays of scores of vendors and non-profit groups.

In the school cafeteria, you can grab a plate of "marsh chicken" for yourself. Oyster fritters and hot dogs will be on the menu for those who can't bring themselves to try a little 'rat.

Tourism info: Dorchester County (Md.) Tourism

CRAWFISH BOIL AND MUSKRAT LEG-EATING WORLD CHAMPIONSHIP

Late February in Cambridge, Md.
Region: Lower Eastern Shore of Maryland

The name pretty much says it all, don't you think? This inspired bit of Eastern Shore wackiness is like icing on the rodent cake of Outdoor Show weekend in Dorchester County, Md. The star attraction once again is a cute little rodent that has been the target of trappers out in the marshlands of Delmarva for too many generations to count--back to Native American times. Local chefs will prepare that muskrat for your dining pleasure in various ways, from bare-bones traditional to modern-day tacos and more. As for the crawfish, they're flown in from Louisiana and served up in traditional Cajun fashion, as well as in sliders and other variations.

Needless to say, libations will be flowing. The music is always outstanding, a mix of blues and classic rock and soul. Be sure to stay through to the culmination of things—that would be the prestigious Muskrat Leg-Eating World Championship competition.

Will a proven past champ take the crown—Chunky? Dirty Legs? Chuckie "Love"? Or will some newcomer rise to the top this year? Hey, that newcomer could be you. All you've got to do is swallow hard and sign up to put your gastrointestinal system to the ultimate test.

Tourism info: Dorchester County (Md.) Tourism

PART TWO: DESTINATIONS
CHAPTER FIVE: EASTERN SHORE
OF VIRGINIA DESTINATIONS

•————— • •●• • —————•

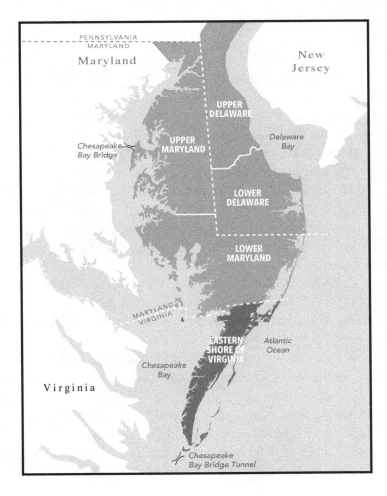

RIDE TO GREENBACKVILLE

The ride through the northeasternmost corner of Virginia's Eastern Shore is quiet as can be nowadays. So much so that it might be hard to imagine the hubbub of the place in the late 1800s.

That's when the Worcester Railroad ran a line down here to the shores of the northern reaches of Chincoteague Bay. Famous Chincoteague Island is on the southern end of that bay. No causeway connected the island to the mainland back then, so that rail line (in combination with steam-powered ferries) opened up access to the island's bountiful supplies of seafood and produce. It also opened up the island to tourism.

Two towns rose in this marshland, both full of folks determined to make the most of these new markets. Both Greenbackville and Franklin City thrived early on, only to fall victim over time to competition from trucks, highways, and other rail lines. Greenbackville is still here, quiet as can be. Franklin City is long gone, except for some pilings and other detritus that might be visible at low tide. (I tell the story of Franklin City in some detail in my book, *You Wouldn't Believe: 44 Strange and Wondrous Delmarva Tales*.)

Greenbackville, the survivor, still has hints of those bustling old glory days. There won't be much in the way of shopping and dining, but there will be charming old houses, narrow streets, waterfront views, and even a rocky little stretch of beach.

Another thing to keep in mind while here: The landscape leading into or out of town along State Line Road (Route 679) was the childhood stomping grounds of Warner Mifflin, an underappreciated American hero who grew up to become a leading (and very early) advocate for the abolition of slavery.

TIP JAR: If you choose to make the journey in or out of

Greenbackville by way of Snow Hill, Md., you'll pass through a couple of other interesting old towns, Girdletree and Stockton. You could stop and explore the E.A. Vaughn Wildlife Management Area along that way, too.

Tourism info: Eastern Shore of Virginia Tourism

Onancock Itinerary

First things first: Stop at Ker Place on the way into this riverfront town. It's home to the Eastern Shore of Virginia Historical Society. Exhibits there will show why this Georgian-style home—it dates to about 1800—ranks as an architectural gem. The broader landscape of Virginia's whole Eastern Shore will come into focus here, too. Old silver is one highlight in the society's collection of artifacts and furnishings. If the scheduling works out, the Eastern Shore Watermen's Museum and the Samuel D. Outlaw Blacksmith Shop belong on your historical hit list as well.

Onancock has a well-deserved reputation as an artists' colony, so spend time in the galleries while wandering the cute downtown. The Historic Onancock School has been remade into a collection of working-artist studies—check that website to see about visiting. If you're spending an evening, see if anything's playing at the North Street Theatre.

From downtown, stroll a few residential blocks to reach the gorgeous Onancock Creek waterfront. There, you'll find an old general store building that currently houses a restaurant serving up fabulous views in addition to meals. If you'll lucky, that scenery will be shrouded in the mist that gives the town its name—Onancock is an old Indian word for "foggy place."

Back out on the highway, you might stop for coffee and browsing at the indie Book Bin. You should also plan to make your way a few miles south to visit Turner Sculpture, a 4,000-square-foot facility that showcases the extraordinary bronze wildlife sculptures of brothers Bill and David Turner.

Tourism info: Eastern Shore of Virginia Tourism

TANGIER ISLAND

Getting to many Chesapeake islands involves crossing a bridge—think Tilghman, Deal, and Hoopers, among others. But Tangier is the real deal, in the sense of taking a 40-minute boat ride out of Crisfield or Onancock. That cruise will give you a whole new understanding of what it means to live in the middle of Chesapeake nowhere.

When Europeans first arrived on the Eastern Shore, they weren't much interested in islands like this. That changed as the population grew and grazing land got harder to find. The first people to hold title to these islands didn't move out there themselves—they shipped livestock out and left the animals to fatten up. Some humans had moved in full time by the time of the Revolutionary War. Both Tangier and nearby Smith Island, Md. had reputations back then as nests of British loyalists, or "picaroons," who behaved more like thieves and pirates than soldiers. Real British soldiers came calling during the War of 1812, famously commandeering Tangier as a camp on their way to the famed Battle of Baltimore.

All this and much more you will learn while perusing the Tangier History Museum. From there, start wandering around—this that ranks among the great cultural gems of the Chesapeake, thanks to the people of Tangier and the one-of-a-kind way of life they've pursued through many generations. Your time here will basically involve a lot of strolling—past homes standing along the island's backbone-like ridge, through the harbor where watermen ply their trades, along a pristine beach, and out beyond for views of sweet marshland and open water. There are places where you can rent kayaks, bikes, and golf carts.

A couple of restaurants serve down-home food. A couple of shops might be open. On a one-day trip, you'll only have a couple of hours before your return ferry departs unless you make special arrangements with some boat or another for a later ride. Stay overnight if you want to watch the watermen get to work in the wee hours of the morning.

Tourism info: Eastern Shore of Virginia Tourism

CHINCOTEAGUE #1: THE MUSEUM

Among the bevy of interesting things to pause over while meandering through the Museum of Chincoteague Island are those famous ponies, Misty and Stormy, who are here in all their taxidermied glory. You'll get in touch as well with stories about fires and floods, ferries and oysters, and a famous lighthouse, too. A favorite for me is learning about Miles Hancock, the most famous of Chincoteague's decoy carvers. He emerged from a rough-and-tumble childhood to become a serial entrepreneur whose exploits as a turtle farmer, market gunner, and hunting guide are almost as celebrated as the primitive folk-art decoys he carved later in life. After his death in 1974, the new people who took over the property where Hancock lived left his old workshop untouched for decades. A few years ago, they donated it to the Museum of Chincoteague, where it has since been moved and reassembled to look just like it did when Mr. Hancock was working his decoy magic. When you visit, it'll feel like he just stepped out to grab a coffee.

Family fun awaits nearby along bustling Maddox Boulevard. Ride ponies and visit the petting zoo at the Chincoteague Pony Center. Make a splash at Maui Jack's Waterpark. Stand in line for ice cream at the famous Island Creamery—it'll be worth it!

Tourism info: Chincoteague Chamber of Commerce and/ or Eastern Shore of Virginia Tourism

CHINCOTEAGUE #2: THE OLD DOWNTOWN

The causeway that links Chincoteague Island with the mainland ranked as a modern marvel back in the early 1920s. Excitement was through the roof on opening day, which turned into a disaster as torrential rains left scores of cars mired in mud overnight. Nothing like that has happened lately, so no worries about crossing over.

Head south of that causeway to visit the old downtown, with its array of art galleries and shops along Main Street. Find your way to the waterfront Robert Reed Park to savor the water views, study up on the historical markers, and admire a dramatic statue of Misty the pony.

When you walk past the old Island Theatre, keep an eye on the sidewalk. When the 1961 Hollywood movie "Misty" opened at this very theater, the famed pony herself strolled through downtown and left those hoof prints in wet concrete. Across the street is a local institution, Sundial Books. Head south from downtown to see the historic old fireman's carnival grounds—the carnival will be up and running in July. Both the serene Chincoteague Island Watermen's Memorial and the famed Beebe Ranch—Misty's old home—are out this way too.

In the opposite direction, north of that causeway, find your way to the itty bitty but fascinating old Captain Timothy Hill House, believed to be the island's oldest surviving home. Keep heading north to reach a cul de sac where you can visit the grave of Captain Joshua L. Chandler and learn about his life—he was struck by lightning in 1877 while serving biscuits to the crew aboard his schooner.

Tourism info: Chincoteague Chamber of Commerce and/ or Eastern Shore of Virginia Tourism

CHINCOTEAGUE #3: THE REFUGE

Hiking, beach, ponies, birding, and more—the Chincoteague National Wildlife Refuge has it all for outdoors lovers. Get the lay of the land by checking out the exhibits and picking up maps and brochures at the Bateman Educational Center. Then head out strolling along one or more of the trails that run through forests and marshlands. You'll be walking in the footsteps of the Pocomoke and Occohannock Indians, who visited the island in nomadic fashion during pre-European times. Most of those trails will involve fabulous shoreline views at one point or another. (One trail leads out to the postcard-pretty Assateague Lighthouse—that beacon has its own section in these pages.)

The refuge boasts a glorious and expansive beach, but take your time on the drive out there, as herons, egrets, and lots of other avian life might be hanging around along the way. Don't think of this as a warm-weather-only destination—the snow geese put on quite a show in the colder months.

In the saving-best-for-last department, keep your eye out for those famous little ponies all year round. If gawking at them is your top priority, then you can look into booking seats aboard one of the several local pony-cruise boat tour operations. As the day draws to a close, leave time to drive the pretty Wildlife Loop, open from 3 p.m. to dusk—hopefully, it will live up to its name.

Tourism info: Chincoteague Chamber of Commerce and/ or Eastern Shore of Virginia Tourism

CHINCOTEAGUE #4: THE ASSATEAGUE LIGHTHOUSE

The first lighthouse built on this Virginia end of Assateague Island went up clear back in the 1830s, but the construction was shoddy, and it lasted just a few short decades. The Assateague Lighthouse that stands today inside of the Chincoteague National Wildlife Refuge was built in 1867 as a replacement. Because of its perch on a bluff above the beach, Assateague Light stands even taller than its imposing 142 feet. The light can be seen by ships from up to 19 miles away.

Nowadays, the beacon does double duty as a functioning navigation aid and an educational tourist attraction. It might be an exhausting one, too—the public is welcome to climb up inside the lighthouse during most weekends of the warmer months. There are 175 steps in that tight circular stairway. While trudging, think about the poor lighthouse keepers early on who had to make the trip once an hour–yes, every day—to keep the light fueled in oil.

The lighthouse had a first-order Fresnel lens in its early days. Invented by a Frenchman, those fascinating devices greatly improved the visibility of beacons in the late 1800s. You won't find that lens waiting at the top of your climb, but you can find it not too far away. It's on display at the nearby Museum of Chincoteague Island.

164

Tourism info: Chincoteague Chamber of Commerce and/ or Eastern Shore of Virginia Tourism

Wallops Flight Facility

While it's historic, this National Aeronautics and Space Administration (NASA) facility is the most futuristic of Delmarva tourism attractions. The rocket-launch center is located right along the road into Chincoteague. Pull in and you'll find a visitors center that offers fun exhibits about those rockets as well as aeronautics, scientific balloons, and other flighty matters.

In addition to learning about current NASA missions and private-sector launches, you'll learn about rich the history of space flight right here on the Virginia shore—those stories go back to the days when experimental monkeys were getting shot into orbit because no one really knew if humans would be able to survive in outer space. Once that question was answered, Wallops played an important role in the tests that led up to the Mercury program—yes, the one that famously sent John Glenn into orbit. More than 16,000 launches have happened at Wallops since its founding in 1945

Check the calendar of events in advance. The visitors center frequently runs kid-friendly educational programs. Oh, and there will be nerdy souvenirs aplenty at the gift shop.

Tourism info: Eastern Shore of Virginia Tourism

Saxis Island

To paraphrase from "The Wizard of Oz": You're not in Chincoteague anymore. This real-deal watermen's community is located on Pocomoke Sound, on the Chesapeake Bay side of the peninsula. Getting there from the Route 13 highway involves turning west toward Saxis instead of east toward Chincoteague. The turn to watch for, Route 695, arrives while passing through Temperanceville.

You'll soon pass through a big swath of marshland, the Saxis Wildlife Management Area. After that comes the "island"—technically, it's a peninsula. That Saxis is thick with history is something you'll learn while visiting the excellent Saxis Island Museum. It's not open a ton of regular hours, so it's best to make an appointment and meet up with a local volunteer history buff.

As of this writing, you'll find a little down-home grill and a tiki bar down on the waterfront. Otherwise, visiting Saxis is mostly a matter of wandering around the harbor and then strolling or driving down this side street and up that narrow road, always on the lookout for scenes that strike your fancy. Chances are, that fancy will end up satisfied.

On the way in or out, watch for a sign pointing the way to Makemie Monument Park. Located in a pretty spot, it honors a pioneering Presbyterian preacher from the turn of the 18th century who also stood up forthrightly (and at great personal cost) for our free-speech rights as well as his faith.

Tourism info: Eastern Shore of Virginia Tourism

DESTINATION PARKSLEY

Parksley didn't take shape slowly over time in the manner of most Delmarva towns. Instead, it came together all at once as a planned community centered along a railroad line that appeared in the late 1800s. Stop first at the Eastern Shore Railway Museum, housed in and around a restored old station chock full of railroading memorabilia. Some classic old railroad cars are parked nearby.

Another tidbit: The team of investors that put Parksley together wasn't homegrown—the founders were mostly Yankees from up north. In another oddity for those times, a woman helped lead the charge. One New York newspaper made a big deal out of Elizabeth Chadbourne's key role in Parksley's founding in an 1893 story headlined "A Live Town Was Founded by a Woman."

The smattering of businesses in the old downtown Parksley includes an old-school five-and-dime, Jaxon's. One online reviewer described the experience there quite well: "Walk into this store, and you are walking into the 1950s when sales clerks were friendly, helpful, knew the merchandise. ... Talk to the salespeople, and you might get a free slice-of-life story about growing up in a small Southern town. This place is really wonderful."

One other bit of advice: Leave time for aimless wandering along the backroads outside of town, whether pedaling or driving.

Tourism info: Eastern Shore of Virginia Tourism

THAT OLD-SCHOOL STUCKEY'S

Many of us who have reached "a certain age" will have fond childhood memories from the glory days of Stuckey's. That Southern-flavored chain of shops functioned as interstate "travel plazas" before anyone knew what such a thing was. For a while, the company's advertising slogan was, "Hey, America ... come on by!"

They were in just about every state of the union there for a while, which is not bad for an operation that started as an open-air roadside stand in Georgia. During my childhood, the bright blue roof of Stuckey's was a welcome site. That was the business you could count on for clean restrooms and fast food served up in sandwich-grill fashion. But they also had old-time candy counters, "world-famous" pecan log rolls, aisles packed with goofy novelty toys, and kitschy souvenirs.

How many of those worthless items did I whine my parents into buying back then? In any case, the point of this reverie is to say that you'll want to keep your eye out while on the Route 13 highway at Mappsville, because an old-school Stuckey's is still up and running there. The address to plug into your phone is 14439 Lankford Hwy., Mappsville.

Tourism info: Eastern Shore of Virginia Tourism

MUTTON HUNK FEN WILDLIFE AREA

The primary reason this wildlife area exists is understandably off limits to the public—it was created to protect a community of plants known as a "fen." The one here at Mutton Hunk is an extra special fen because it's thriving in a rare type of freshwater wetland that pops up sometimes even at the edge of a salty coast. Five rare-for-Virginia plants are found in the fen acres here, along with lots of other vegetation of interest.

But the preserve near Mappsville has 300 or so non-fen acres, too. The place has done duty over the years as a dairy farm, a tomato farm, and a soybean farm, but the acreage is now managed to promote bird habitat. Avian life is abundant here all year round, but Mutton Hunk is really hopping during migration months. Two trails are open to visitors, one leading out to a view of a big stretch of saltmarsh on the edge of Gargathy Bay. You'll be able to see a couple of barrier islands from there. The other trail runs along White's Creek, where lots of wading birds like to spend their hunting hours.

Also, my apologies: I do not know the answer to the burning question of how "mutton hunk" got its name.

Tourism info: Eastern Shore of Virginia Tourism

ACCOMAC ITINERARY

Your starting point in the seat of Accomack County will be obvious upon arrival, that glorious old town square. A red-brick courthouse there dates to 1899. Nearby is a county clerk's office that houses records that date back to the 1660s, the second-oldest uninterrupted set of such documents in the country (after the nearby town of Eastville). The most famous structure on the square is the Debtor's Prison, a small and rather nondescript brick affair built in 1783 and used in the early 1800s as a lockup for folks who fell behind on their finances and couldn't pay a court fee or a tax bill.

After wandering the square, stroll hither and yon along nearby Back and Front streets. You'll find some fabulous old houses, sweet gardens, and several church buildings that have remarkable connections with key figures in the history of the Baptist, Methodist, and Presbyterian faiths. You might find a restaurant here in town, but you might not—nearby Onley is the place to go for old-school diners, Latino food trucks, and other options. One last recommendation: If you are in the mood for backroads, wander along Drummondtown Road, which leads to the next destination here.

And yes, the city and county have the same pronunciation, but slightly different spellings.

Tourism info: Eastern Shore of Virginia Tourism

WACHAPREAGUE

Also known as the "Little City by the Sea," Wachapreague still has the look and feel of an old fishing village. While walking around, it will be easy to imagine Wachapreague's century-old glory days. During those roaring '20s, the town had a dozen shops, a movie theater, and a pool hall among its amenities. The elegant old Wachapreague Hotel stood near where the Island House restaurant is today. The staff there used to serve elegant al fresco dinners out on Parramore Island, visible on the horizon. During those same years, Prohibition-era bootleggers famously took shipments of illegal booze and repackaged the liquid contraband into fish barrels.

The town still does a good amount of tourism trade, mostly among anglers who rent boats and/or guides during their stay. If you are not among the fisherpeople, the visit here will be mostly about strolling or driving about, gawking at this old store, that old church, and the house up around the next corner. Either coming or going, take the long way back to the highway by riding along Drummondtown Road through Locustville—historian Kirk Mariner quite rightly described the streetscape at that old stagecoach stop as the closest thing you'll find to how things looked hereabouts during the Civil War.

Tourism info: Eastern Shore of Virginia Tourism

RIDE TO HARBORTON

Along the bayside the ride from pretty little Belle Haven up to Harborton and gorgeous Pungoteague Creek you will be traveling a backroads landscape thick with African American heritage. The road you're looking for here goes by a couple of different numbers (178 and 718) and runs by several different names (Boston, Bobtown, Savageville) on its way up to Onancock. From Belle Haven, you'll pass through Craddockville and then into Boston.

That little settlement has its roots in a gift of 200 acres that plantation owner Abel West gave to his slaves after freeing them in the exceedingly early year of 1805. West wanted that land to be held "in common" by those former slaves as a "place of Refuge." You'll pass the old Boston School and a pair of historic black churches on the way to Pungoteague.

The area north and west of that outpost is probably where the free black man Anthony Johnson operated a farm in the 1600s that he named "Angola," presumably after his African homeland. By turning on Route 180, you'll wander north through that landscape and up into Harborton, where you can relax for a bit with the sweet waterfront views at the boat ramp. A little Harborton history museum is open only on Saturday afternoons as of this writing, so either time your trip right or call to see about an appointment.

Tourism info: Eastern Shore of Virginia Tourism

RIDE TO WILLIS WHARF

On the oceanside east of Exmore, the fishing village of Willis Wharf makes for a quick but splendid little detour. The scenery will be outstanding as you follow Willis Wharf Road into town, curving as the road bends to the right past the striking old E.L. Willis store building and then a big aquaculture facility. You'll wind over a little bridge and then past a boat ramp on the way into the far part of town.

That area is home to a neighborhood known as Little Hog Island. Six of the houses along Hog Island Lane were moved to this block from the storied barrier island of that name. People lived out on that island back in Revolutionary War times. By the late 1800s, the island was home to the thriving town of Broadwater and ranked as a famous travel destination for rich outdoorsy types, with five lavish hunt clubs. President Grover Cleveland went hunting there. Everyone left the island during an early 1900s run of terrible storms that accelerated erosion problems on the island. They all moved to the mainland, making this neighborhood a little remnant of those island glory days.

On the way back keep your eye on the tidal flats in addition to the glorious horizon. In spring and fall, migrating whimbrels like to cavort there in big numbers.

Tourism info: Eastern Shore of Virginia Tourism

BROWNSVILLE PRESERVE

Pack up your binoculars for the stroll that awaits along the birding trail at the Brownsville Preserve, which is on the oceanside of Nassawadox along Route 608. The small trailhead parking area at 11332 Brownsville Rd. will put you in position to set off on a 3.5-mile round-trip hike through woods, meadows, and marshlands, all managed by the Nature Conservancy to be as friendly as possible to birds and other wildlife. Trail guides should be available at a kiosk in that parking area.

You'll feel like you're walking through a timeless refuge of nature, but the reality is different. For more than three centuries, the land here was in the hands of a single family, the Upshurs, and did duty as farmland and a trading center. From a colonial-era wharf on Brownsville Creek, the Upshurs shipped corn up the Atlantic to markets as far away as New York and New England.

Tourism info: Eastern Shore of Virginia Tourism

BARRIER ISLANDS CENTER

Several times here I have mentioned the storied barrier islands
that rise off of the coast of Virginia's Eastern Shore. The best
place to delve into the nature, history, and culture of those marvels is located just off the Route 13 highway at Machipongo.
The Barrier Islands Center is one of my all-time favorite small
museums. Located in a historic old "almshouse," BIC delivers a
first-rate introduction to the incredible stories that have unfolded
over the centuries on those thin strips of land.

Through an always engaging mix of film, artifacts, and
wall panels, you will learn about the resourceful communities
that thrived out there, the hunting and fishing clubs that became
famous outdoorsy tourism destinations, and the bold "wreckers"
who responded to ships in distress even before there was a fed-
eral life-saving service. The one-two punch of storms and erosion
eventually drove residents onto the mainland in the early 1900s,
but this museum will bring those communities back to life in your
mind's eye.

Tourism info: Eastern Shore of Virginia Tourism

EASTVILLE ITINERARY

The primary attraction here is a courthouse square that's as
historic as it gets when it comes to European settlement on the
Delmarva Peninsula. The seat of Northampton County, Eastville
is home to the country's oldest continuous set of court records,
which have miraculously survived the dangers of fire, flood, war,
and human carelessness since clear back in 1632. Court sessions
back then were held in a local tavern by judges who traveled from
outpost to outpost on horseback.

The "new" Courthouse here, which dates to the 1890s, ranks as an architectural toddler compared with the "old" Courthouse. Parts of that latter building date to the 1730s. An old "Clerk's Office" dates to before the Revolution as well. Restoration of an "Old Jail" was in process at the time of this writing. Some of the buildings are open to the public during weekday business hours. A stroll along the surrounding blocks will also be worthwhile, as they boast a good number of sweet old houses. You won't find much in the way of creature comforts here—head back to the highway or down to Cheriton if all that strolling leaves you hungry.

Tourism info: Eastern Shore of Virginia Tourism

SAVAGE DUNES NATURAL AREA

Find your way into the countryside near Eastville along Savage Neck Road (Route 634) and keep going until you reach a pull-off at a little parking area for Savage Neck Dunes Natural Area Preserve. At this 300-acre slice of Delmarva heaven, you'll need to take a mile-or-so stroll through maritime forestlands and then climb up and over some gentle sand dunes in order to reach an expansive and pristine beach looking out over the broad Chesapeake Bay. Maybe pack a picnic?

If you're a history buff, do a little advance reading about Thomas Savage, the man behind the name here. He arrived, flying solo, at historic Jamestown at the tender age of 13. Captain John Smith ordered him to live with local Indians in a 1600s version of a cultural-exchange program. He fled that tribe when war broke out, then worked as a translator, fur trader, and farmer. The reason this land bears his name is that he received it as a gift from a friend, the Indian chief Esmy Shichans—a guy everyone knew as

the "Laughing King."
      Tourism info: Eastern Shore of Virginia Tourism

CAPE CHARLES ITINERARY

Perched near the southernmost tip of the Delmarva Peninsula is
one of the Eastern Shore's most charming small towns. Get the
lay of the land by stopping to see the exhibits at the Cape Charles
Museum and Welcome Center. There, you'll learn how Cape
Charles took shape much later than most Delmarva towns, rising
only as a railroad line arrived in the 1880s. That railroad connected people and produce with steamships and barges that then
sailed across the Chesapeake Bay to Norfolk. You'll see steamship and ferry models, admire old railroad cars, and visit a reconstructed old railroad station.

      Pick up a walking-tour brochure while there, because
Cape Charles is a strolling joy. Both its downtown and its residential streets have a charming turn-of-the-20th-century vibe in
architecture and streetscapes. You might dawdle most of the day
away in the array of downtown shops, eateries, and galleries. But
be sure to leave enough time for a pair of sweet strolls, one along
the town's expansive beach and the other over to Central Park.
      Tourism info: Eastern Shore of Virginia Tourism

KIPTOPEKE STATE PARK

Named after an old country estate that in turn took its name from
an Accohannock Indian chief, Kiptopeke State Park covers 562
acres just south of Cape Charles. A popular fishing and birding
spot, it's got five-plus miles of hiking and cycling trails, as well
as a little beach.

The view from that beach is a strange and wondrous affair, as the humongous arc of a jetty that lies off in the distance is made from a curved line of eerie-looking, half-sunken ghost ships. Built with concrete hulls during World War II—other materials were in short supply then—the vessels served as wartime supply ships, then became obsolete. They were put mothballed for a while, then moved here to protect a ferry terminal (which is now long gone) from the vagaries of weather and waves. Today, the ghost ships of Kiptopeke serve both as a bizarre sightseeing attraction and as a big draw for fish populations that love underwater nooks and crannies.

A great time to visit is during migration season. This end of the Virginia shore is like the skinny part of a funnel—a gazillion birds pass through this funnel before spreading out across wider swaths of land that are available in other parts of their journeys.

Tourism info: Eastern Shore of Virginia Tourism

EASTERN SHORE OF VIRGINIA NATIONAL WILDLIFE REFUGE

At the 1,100-acre Eastern Shore of Virginia National Wildlife Refuge, you can stroll trails, climb up observation platforms, and go birding from your car along a network of roads. They'll even rent you binoculars if you forget to bring a pair. The visitor center there has interesting exhibits, including the story of how this property used to be an air force facility called Fort John Custis.

If you check the schedule, you might be able to sign on for a tour of the nearby Fisherman Island National Wildlife Refuge—they are usually available on Saturdays between October and February. During a guided two-mile stroll, you'll learn not just about the 200-acre island's natural wonders, but also how it served back in the 1800s as a quarantine station for immigrants and during both world wars as an artillery station protecting the mainland. If you are a sunrise aficionado, you might try the Marsh Overlook Trail.

Two more walking trails are available at the nearby Magothy Bay Natural Area Preserve, a 400-plus-acre stretch of land that has been transformed in recent decades from farmland into another birding hotspot.

Tourism info: Eastern Shore of Virginia Tourism

Cruising Seaside Drive

For a great backroads drive on the lower end of the peninsula, find your way to Seaside Road (Route 600) as it parallels Route 13 on the oceanside. Be sure to make the turn into Oyster for a glimpse at another timeless old fishing village. On one side of the water is a boat ramp and marina where you can check out the local fishing activity. On the other side of the water along Sunnyside Road is a relatively new strolling option, the Oyster Village Horse Island Trail. Hopefully, the sweet old plank-on-a-rope swing will still be hanging from a tree on the day you reach the end of that stroll.

Back on Seaside Road, keep a close eye out on the oceanside when you get around 20190 Seaside Road—it's easy to miss the Brinkley Nature Preserve entrance, but well worth a little aggravation to get there. Named for a local birding enthusiast, the preserve features a large, deep lake that draws lots of ducks, grebes, gulls, and other birds, especially during the winter months. A little farther up the road is Seaview Farm. Organic farming is done here on lands surrounded by woods and marshlands that are protected through a conservation easement with the Nature Conservancy—visitors are welcome to stroll the short trails there. This entrance is easy to miss, too. It's near 18119 Seaside Road, but the trick is to find an oceanside pull off about 100 yards south of a house that has a small sign out front painted on an oar, reading "Seaview."

North of that, keep your eyes out for Indiantown Neck Road, Route 631. That road ends at Indiantown Recreational Park, which has a little hiking trail through lands that housed the Gingaskin Indian settlement in pre-Columbian times. Here, too, was the only Indian reservation ever established on the Eastern Shore of Virginia, set up in 1640. After that, stay on Seaside Drive and enjoy the scenery on a lovely ride into the town of Nassawadox.

Tourism info: Eastern Shore of Virginia Tourism

THE GARDENS AT EYRE HALL

The colonial gem of a home called Eyre Hall is open for interior tours only once a year during the springtime Eastern Shore of Virginia Garden Tour (see that entry in the events section), but visitors are welcome other days to stop at the estate near Cheriton and stroll through the family graveyard and gardens that rank among the oldest in the country. They were planted back when Thomas Jefferson was president. Inside the striking brick garden wall are evocative little paths and centuries-old boxwoods and crepe myrtles.

Take a break on one of the benches there and let your mind's eye wander in time. The estate's history dates clear back to the 1660s, and the property remains in the hands of the same family who "patented" it back then—they are now at 12 generations and counting. The bricks in the garden wall were supposedly brought over from England as ballast on a ship. The ruins of an old orangery add to the awe-inspiring atmosphere.

Tourism info: Eastern Shore of Virginia Tourism

Shore Bets!

CHAPTER SIX:
LOWER EASTERN SHORE OF MARYLAND DESTINATIONS

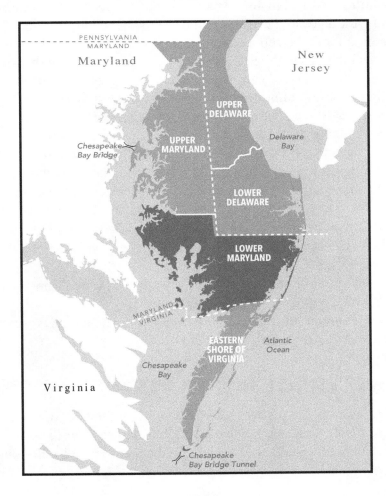

OCEAN CITY

Just go. Wander around. It'll be fun.

If you're on the south end of town, by the inlet and the boardwalk, get the lay of the land at the Ocean City Life-Saving Station Museum, which serves up lots of old shipwreck legends in addition to local history. History-laden Trimpers Rides amusement park dates to the 1890s and remains in the hands of its founding family. Deep inside there, you will find a priceless old carousel that dates to 1912 and ranks as a survivor from the so-called "golden age of carousels," when immigrant artisans used all manner of building-trades projects—even kiddie rides like this—as artistic canvases. French fries, salt-water taffy, chintzy souvenir shops—just walk the boardwalk.

Heading north along Baltimore Boulevard and the Coastal Highway is a long parade of mini-golf, family amusements, shops, and eateries. Take the Route 90 bridge across the water to find your way to pretty little Isle of Wight Park. Up on the north end of town, be sure to take the time to stroll gorgeous Northside Park. At Christmastime, that is the site of the town's famous Winterfest of Lights.

Hey, did I mention that the town has a 10-mile-long beach that's kinda popular in the summer months?

Tourism info: Ocean City (Md.) Tourism and/or Worcester County (Md.) Tourism

ASSATEAGUE ISLAND

Again, just go. It's a sweet ride from West Ocean City down Route 611 to Assateague Island, which is named after the Native American tribe that once lived in the area. The 37-mile-long stretch of sandy beach, swaying grasses, and shady forest is best known as home to a herd of diminutive wild ponies. No one knows for sure how those ponies arrived, but they now roam freely along beaches and roadways, chomping up grasses while looking as adorable as all get out. (It goes without saying, but still: Don't feed the horses, and don't mess with the horses.)

Access is available through both a state park and a national seashore. Either way, you will find much more than those ponies to gawk at. There's that glorious beach, of course. There are also hiking trails, cycling routes, and paddling opportunities. Various signs along the way will introduce you to the ecology and natural history of the island.

On the mainland is a visitors center with interesting exhibits. In the state park be sure to find your way to the Rackliffe Plantation House, the 18th-century abode of Capt. Charles Rackliffe. It overlooks Sinepuxent Bay.

Tourism info: Worcester County (Md.) Tourism

BERLIN ITINERARY

A short ride from Ocean City, Berlin stands in the top ranks of Delmarva downtowns in lots of categories—pretty historic streetscape, dining and shopping options, and stories to tell. Stop at the Calvin Taylor House on the way into town to meet the cast of interesting characters who've called this place home. They include Man o' War, the most famous racehorse of them all; naval hero Steven Decatur; actress Linda Harrison, a onetime Delmarva Poultry Queen who starred in the original "Planet of the Apes;" gospel composer Charles Tindley, whose "Stand By Me" morphed through the years in the civil rights anthem, "We Shall Overcome. You'll learn, too, about Berlin's starring role as the backdrop for the Hollywood megahit "Runaway Bride."

In the heart of downtown, you'll find lots of antiques and boutiques and dessert stops and good eats. Have a drink on the porch at the old Atlantic Hotel. Go see first-rate glassblower Jeffrey Auxer at work. Don't miss out on the Mermaid Museum, an idiosyncratic little museum dedicated to those mythical denizens of the deep. Keep an eye out there for the little Cheeto on display. Trust me on that last one—I don't want to ruin the surprise here.

Tourism info: Worcester County (Md.) Tourism

Snow Hill Itinerary

Snow Hill has endured its share of lean times through the centuries, but the town always seems to bounce back. The current upswing is thanks in large part to pioneering entrepreneurs like Ann Coates, whose Bishop's Stock gallery helped spark an artsy turn for a town with deep roots in sailing ships, timbering, and farming. New shops and eateries have been popping up regularly in recent years—a coffee shop here, a specialty candy shop there, and a sprawling toy store around the corner. The town boasts remarkable old architecture, most of it dating to another bounce-back era—the town's recovery from a pair of devastating fires in the late 1800s.

A walking-tour brochure should be readily available around town. Be sure to stroll down to pretty Sturgis Park on the Pocomoke River. Along Church Street one of the houses to gawk at is the Queen Anne-style gem that one-time governor of Maryland John Walter Smith built for his family back in 1889. Nearby is the commanding All Hallows Episcopal Church, which went up in the 1750s.

The little Julia Purnell Museum is another must-stop. It

has an idiosyncratic collection of local ephemera in addition to telling the story of its namesake—a woman whose journey to artistic renown went into overdrive at the age of 85 when she landed in a wheelchair after a bad fall. Some 100 of her quilts, dolls, and applique compositions are in the collection.

Tourism info: Worcester County (Md.) Tourism

POCOMOKE RIVER STATE PARK

Pocomoke River State Park is the best place on the Lower Eastern Shore to explore the remnants of what was once a 50,000-plus-acre swath of swamp that stretched up into southern Delaware. The star attraction here is the swamp-loving bald cypress tree, a strange creature that looks like a pine but drops all of its needle-like leaves every fall and is often surrounded by knobby little "knees" rising out of the ground.

A couple of historians have speculated that dark and spooky remnants of the old cypress swamp—there is another up in Delaware's Trap Pond State Park—might be as close as we can get to seeing something that looks similar to what Captain John Smith saw on Delmarva in the early 1600s. In 1809, one traveler dubbed the dark swamp "one of the most frightful labyrinths you can imagine."

No wonder the place served over the centuries as a hiding place for everyone from British loyalists and runaway slaves to moonshiners and criminals on the run. Hiking, paddling, cycling—it'll be a day of outdoorsy joy.

Tourism info: Worcester County (Md.) Tourism

FURNACE TOWN AND NASSAWANGO CREEK

The story behind Furnace Town Historic Site is a fascinating entrepreneurial affair rooted in the natural resources of the vast cypress swamp that dominated this landscape for centuries. Such swamps are beehives of biochemical activity, and one byproduct of those processes is "bog iron," a goopy substance that with a little help from human ingenuity can be turned into iron. Local farm families were the first to get those processes going on this land just north of Snow Hill, but bigger businessmen soon moved in and launched a furnace operation so big that 300 people lived in a company town during the mid-1800s. The ruins of that furnace are still standing. The surrounding "historical village" boasts a restored blacksmith shop, a one-room schoolhouse, a woodworking shop, a church, and other structures from various historical periods.

Keep your eyes peeled here for the entrance to the Paul Liefer Trail, which leads through the Nature Conservancy's Nassawango Creek Preserve. More adventurous hikers should find their way online to a map of the various other trails that run through the preserve's 9,000-plus acres. The restoration work here has led to the reappearance of wild orchids, including white-fringed and crested-yellow varieties that bloom for a few short weeks in the summer months.

Ambitious hikers should look up the Algonquin Cross County Trail. It's 12 miles long, with one trailhead located north of Furnace Town along Snow Hill Road.

Tourism info: Worcester County (Md.) Tourism

POCOMOKE CITY ITINERARY

Housed in a sprawling former car dealership in the heart of downtown Pocomoke City, the Delmarva Discovery Museum delivers a first-rate introduction to the historical, cultural, and natural wonders of the region. Your journey through the centuries here will run from Native American times through steamboats, railroads, and right on up to modern times. Crawl into a beaver lodge, learn about a cypress swamp, and explore the world of those old steamboats.

One thing for sure: You'll want to spend quality time with the museum's pair of cute-as-a-button river otters. Their names are Mac and Tuck.

Cross Market Street to visit Cypress Park and stroll a 1.5-mile-long nature trail that winds around a pond. Also right nearby is the Sturgis One Room School, which tells the story of African American education during segregation times. Downtown Pocomoke City offers a modest collection of shopping and dining options. One good time to visit is during their Fourth Friday block party festivities in the warmer months. Farther up Market Street is the appointment-only Costen House Museum, the former abode of a physician and mayor who arrived in town back in Civil War times.

Tourism info: Worcester County (Md.) Tourism

THE RUINS OF COVENTRY

If you head north from Pocomoke City into Somerset County along Route 13, take the left onto Route 667 (Rehobeth Road) and you will soon be winding this way and that before turning onto Coventry Parish Road and coming upon the ruins of an old church by that name.

Just three brick walls remain standing at Coventry Parish, which was built in the late 1780s. Those post-revolutionary years were tumultuous times in American religious history. The British Anglican Church that formerly ruled the roost in Maryland fell on hard times due to its association with the losing side. This building was part of the effort to reinvent that faith as an all-American institution, the Episcopal Church. Folks worshipped at Coventry for a century before abandoning the place in the late 1800s.

The nearby Rehobeth Presbyterian Church is chock full of history as well. Believed to be the country's oldest Presbyterian church building in continuous use, it was erected in 1706. The "Father of American Presbyterianism," Francis Makemie, probably preached here.

Tourism info: Somerset County (Md.) Tourism

CRISFIELD ITINERARY

First things first: Just drive to the waterfront, stroll out onto the dock, and look around.

Welcome to a town that claims—and not without reason—the grand title of "Crab Capital of the World." Then head to the J. Millard Tawes Historical Museum to get in touch with the stories that Crisfield has to tell. Those stories will have a maritime bent, as this is a place built on shipbuilding, crabbing, and oystering.

Make arrangements through the Tawes Museum in advance if you want to visit the Ward Brothers Workshop, which is where Lemuel and Steve Ward famously help turn the workmanlike craft of decoy carving into a cherished art form.

For a working-class Eastern Shore breakfast (or other meal) in a timeless atmosphere, find your way to Gordon's Confectionary. You'll have more upscale eateries to choose from if you prefer, as well as some modest shopping options. Be sure to check out painter Michael Rosato's mural tribute to the seafood workers of Crisfield. Perhaps stop in the Corbin Art Gallery as well. You might cap off the day by watching the sunset from itty-bitty Wellington Beach.

Tourism info: Somerset County (Md.) Tourism

JANES ISLAND STATE PARK

Located just outside Crisfield, Janes Island State Park is a modest affair if you stick to the mainland. There, you will find campsites, cabins, picnic areas, a park store, and a little nature center. It's a swell place to bring a little picnic and take a little stroll, but not much else.

The real action here is out on the water, whether by paddleboard or kayak or boat. The park encompasses some 3,000 acres of saltmarsh across pretty Daugherty Creek. There are 30 miles of marked water trails out along that creek and its tributaries, with most of those miles reasonably well sheltered from the wind. The marshes will likely be full of birds and other wildlife. Deer have been known to swim from the mainland out to those marshes. If you're paddling, you'll be able to land on pristine, isolated beaches. And yes, kayak, canoe, and paddleboard rentals are available.

Tourism info: Somerset County (Md.) Tourism

DEAL ISLAND AND THE ROAD TO RUMBLEY

On the road to Deal Island (Route 363), you will pass through Dames Quarter—that's a gussied-up version of "Damned Quarter," its original name in rougher and tumbler times gone by. Find your way there along narrow Riley Roberts Road into the Deal Island Wildlife Management Area, a 13,000-acre hiking, paddling, fishing, and hunting gem.

Deal Island, too, has a gussied-up name—it was "Devil's Island" in those rougher days. Today, it's an old-school watermen's community, with most houses lined up along a thin backbone of high ground that ranks as "high" only in comparison with all the other land here. Stop at the Skipjack Heritage Museum to learn more about those watermen, their families, and their ways. Stroll the grounds at St. John's Methodist Church and visit its little Joshua Thomas Chapel. That chapel honors a fascinating 19th century preacher known as the "Parson of the Islands."

Otherwise, just stroll docks full of workboats, watch the locals unload the day's catch, grab a sandwich at the old-time country store near the harbor, and think about the fact that the scenes and rituals of everyday island life that unfold in front of you here are ones that really haven't changed very much for centuries now.

If you want to visit an even more remote watermen's community, find the route through Fairmount (where you can wander the grounds of the old Fairmount Academy) and out to the town of Rumbley. As of this writing, there was a tiki bar waiting at the end of that backroads adventure.

Tourism info: Somerset County (Md.) Tourism

THE HEART OF SALISBURY

A transformation is well underway in downtown Salisbury. Not too many years ago, the streets here were home mostly to offices for lawyers, accountants, and other service professionals, but recent years have seen new shops and restaurants starting to pop up. The city has made a big commitment to adding a residential component to the mix. A great time to visit is during the popular Third Friday festivities in the warmer months.

You can stroll along a recently completed little riverwalk. Several art galleries are up and running, including an always adventurous one run by Salisbury University. Find your way to the residential streets on the north side of Route 50 to tour Poplar Hill Mansion, which dates to the late 1700s, and to visit the historic Parsons Cemetery.

Head down busy Route 13 to find your way to Salisbury University. On campus there, stop in the Guerrieri Academic Commons—there are always interesting exhibits up in the lobby. Upstairs are more exhibits on historical themes from the Nabb Research Center for Delmarva History and Culture. Nearby in Perdue Hall is the Franklin P. Perdue Museum of Business and Entrepreneurship—it tells the story of the Delmarva poultry industry, as seen through the founding and growth of Perdue Farms. There are two art galleries on campus as well—the University Gallery in Fulton Hall and The Electronic Gallery in Conway Hall.

Tourism info: Wicomico County (Md.) Tourism

WARD MUSEUM AND CITY PARK

Most folks think of birding as an outdoors adventure, but you can also find spectacular birds in the climate-controlled confines of the Ward Museum of Wildfowl Art in Salisbury, Md. Home to one of the world's top collections of carved decoys, the museum takes its name from a pair of brothers—Lem and Steve Ward—who ran a barbershop in Crisfield, Md. while turning out a steady stream of world-class work in this fascinating artistic subculture. There is no better place to get acquainted with that subculture.

You can enjoy the great outdoors right nearby at City Park. The trail there tracks a winding river and takes you through the fun little Salisbury Zoo, with its signature pink flamingos. The back story of the park is fascinating. While walking, your shoes will be stepping atop what used to be the bottom of kidney-shaped Humphrey's Lake, which covered 40 acres and stretched from here on the east side of town all the way up the edge of downtown. For a century and a half, Humphrey's Lake was a central feature of life in Salisbury—recreation, baptisms, scenery. The dam collapsed in 1909, draining the lake and leading eventually to the creation of the park.

Tourism info: Wicomico County (Md.) Tourism

PEMBERTON HISTORICAL PARK

This 262-acre gem on the southwestern outskirts of Salisbury serves up a mix of strolling, scenery, and history. A tree-lined gravel lane leads into the property where Isaac Handy built Pemberton Hall in 1741 as the centerpiece of his plantation. That house still stands. Several replica outbuildings add to the authenticity of the scene here, as does a run of distinctive "snake" fencing straight out of history books.

The landscape here was quite different in Handy's time. The forestland now standing between the house and the Wicomico River wasn't there, for instance. When Handy built his house, he had a clear view of the river from his front door, which faced the water because that's where all the action was—overland roads were iffy and little used in his day. Across the water, an old Tondotank Indian village was still standing. Here on Handy's property, enslaved African Americans were toiling away in bondage.

The grounds at Pemberton Manor are open every day, but the interior is open only on occasional weekends, so you will need to check on that schedule. But you'll definitely want to dawdle for quite some time along the park's 4.5 miles of hiking trails. They run through shaded forests, along itty bitty streams, and atop elevated wooden walkways. If you take the History Trail, keep an eye out for the remains of an ancient wharf on the river that dates to Handy's time—it might be visible at low tide.

Tourism info: Wicomico County (Md.) Tourism

SMITH ISLAND

Like Tangier Island in Virginia, Smith Island will give you a whole new notion of what it means to live out in the middle of Chesapeake nowhere. The only way to get there from the Eastern Shore involves a 45-minute boat ride from Crisfield. That cruise will leave you disembarking on a three-by-five-mile splotch of land that's home to 200 hardy souls living in three tiny towns. Folks have been living out here since the 1600s.

You will do fine with a day trip, but staying overnight gives a fuller sense for this one-of-a-kind place, especially if you wake yourself up before the sun rises to watch the island coming to life and the watermen getting about their work.

Be sure to visit the Smith Island Cultural Center and Cavalry Methodist Church. In addition to lots of strolling around to soak up the atmosphere, you should be able to rent kayaks and bicycles and grab some down-home meals. Be warned, though: The restaurants close early, so you will either need to eat supper super early or get takeout and put it in the fridge. Don't forget to order some Smith Island Cake—it's Maryland's official state dessert.

If you do stay overnight, check in advance with the host at your rental about the possibility of signing up for an expedition or some unique experience with one of the locals.

Tourism info: Somerset County (Md.) Tourism

PRINCESS ANNE ITINERARY

The seat of Somerset County is chock full of gorgeous buildings—some 300 of them are included in the Princess Anne Historic District on the National Register. You'll be able to tour one of them, as the 10,000-square-foot Neo-Classical Teackle Mansion—it dates to the early 1800s—is now operated by the Somerset County Historical Society.

Nearby is a small but pretty downtown. Make your way to the corner of Washington and Somerset streets to check out a very cool and very old boxwood garden. Be sure to admire (and perhaps dine at) the Old Washington Hotel. The town is also home to the University of Maryland Eastern Shore, a historically black college that dates its history back to the 1880s. Students there were at the forefront of an interesting chapter in the civil rights movement that unfolded here.

Back out on the Route 13 highway, find your way to the Somerset County Visitors Center, which is home to the new

Burgess Rural Living Center displaying a fascinating collection of farm-life artifacts from across the centuries. If you want to enjoy a bit of green space, Manokin River Park is located north of downtown.

Tourism info: Somerset County (Md.) Tourism

WHITEHAVEN AND THE FERRIES

Southwest of Pemberton Park the Wicomico River opens up in winding fashion on its journey toward the Chesapeake Bay. Find your way to Whitehaven Road (Route 352), which will end in the town of that name. Here, a little car ferry shuttles vehicles across the river. Ferries of one type or another have been running here since back in colonial times.

The three-story Whitehaven Hotel (1810) is a gorgeous remnant of times gone by. Accounts of travelers stopping at the hotel grace the pages of a couple famous old novels about the region, The Entailed Hat and River of Rogues. As of this writing, the place is a privately owned B&B. The stroll up into the heart of town is quite pleasant.

Wicomico County also operates a second ferry service a little way upriver—that one is called the Upper Ferry. You can cross on one and circle back via the other. Or you can wander the backroads on the other side and find your way down to Princess Anne or back up to Salisbury on the Route 13 highway.

Tourism info: Wicomico County (Md.) Tourism

ROARING POINT AND NANTICOKE TOWNS

Speaking of the Nanticoke River, the Wicomico County side of that waterway is chock full of scenic charms as well. Find your way to the spectacularly named town of Bivalve and stroll around pretty Cedar Hill Park. During the winter trapping season, the West Side Volunteer Fire Company here famously holds a community supper featuring a main course of muskrat. Outside the firehouse is the restored hull of an old log canoe, the *Wm. McKinley.*

Head south toward the town of Nanticoke, stopping at two beaches along the way. First up is itty bitty Cove Road Beach, with its photogenic remains of an old pier. Southbound again, keep an eye out for the sharp right turn that leads into Roaring Point Park. A modest little path from the parking area there leads out to a gorgeous expanse of sunset-friendly beach that runs for nearly a full mile.

When you come back north, you might want to find your way to another gem of a backroads town, Tyaskin. There, you can visit a pair of parks on pretty Wetipquin Creek, one at the site of the long-gone Tyaskin Wharf, where steamboats used to stop, and the other is just east of town, farther up the creek.

Tourism info: Wicomico County (Md.) Tourism

VIENNA AND ELLIOTTS ISLAND

The little town of Vienna has been around through a big sweep of history. The local Indians who had a settlement hereabouts received a visit from Captain John Smith himself. A town popped up in colonial times. Stroll the sweet park on the Nanticoke River waterfront, and check out the old 1768 Custom House. Just north of town is Historic Handsell, an 18th-century brick gem where you'll also find a meticulously reconstructed Native American longhouse. The house is open only occasionally, but the grounds are dotted with informative exhibit panels.

Check your gas gauge before heading south on Elliotts Island Road. The round trip to that island covers 40 miles. No shops, no gas stations, no restrooms, just gorgeous cruising. A bigwig with the Nature Conservancy once had this to say about the scenery here: "It is one of the great natural areas on the East Coast. Those marshes are some of the great coastal wilderness we have left." The birding can be amazing, and the island is thick with history. Wander the grounds at pretty Elliott's Island Methodist Church. Make your way out to the marina for more gorgeous views. Then savor that scenery all over again on the ride back.

Perhaps find your way to Layton's Chance winery to cap off the adventure?

Tourism info: Dorchester County (Md.) Tourism

CAMBRIDGE ITINERARY

The seat of Dorchester County has been on the comeback trail long enough now to deliver a healthy array of shopping and dining diversions in a downtown where cool old buildings give off more of an urban vibe than other Delmarva towns. Most famously among beer lovers, this is HQ for the popular RAR brewery. Supposedly, a distillery is on the way—perhaps it will be there when you arrive.

Take the scenic stroll down High Street to the waterfront and check out the Choptank River Lighthouse, where you can climb up inside to see various exhibits during the warmer months.

Check the schedule of public cruises aboard *Skipjack Nathan*, as it docks out at Long Wharf too.

A trio of attractions back downtown celebrate the life and accomplishments of Dorchester native Harriet Tubman of Underground Railroad fame—a statue in front of the courthouse, the small-but-fascinating Harriet Tubman Museum and Education Center, and, behind that, the famous "Take My Hand" mural by artist Michael Rosato. Download the Pine Street Walking Tour brochure (or pick one up at the local visitor center) to explore a National Register corridor that's thick with African American history. If you want to see a classic old-time grocery store, head up to Simmons Center Market—they've been around for more than 80 years. The Richardson Maritime Museum was in transition from one spot to another at this writing, but perhaps they'll be up and running in their new digs by the time you visit.

Tourism info: Dorchester County (Md.) Tourism

HARRIET TUBMAN UNDERGROUND RAILROAD VISITOR CENTER

More a museum than a "visitor center," this exploration of the life and times of an American hero stands in the countryside below Cambridge, in the midst of the landscape where Harriet Tubman was born into slavery and spent many of her younger years. The design, exhibits, and grounds are first-rate in every way, as you'd expect from a joint undertaking of the National Park Service and the Maryland Department of Natural Resources. If you have to choose just one Tubman site, this is the winner.

As long as you're here, however, you might as well venture a few miles over to see the Bucktown Village Store, which is where young Harriet suffered a near-fatal head injury in a confrontation with a white man. That head injury had a huge impact on her later work as a champion of freedom. And since you'll drive through Cambridge on the way in and out, you might as well visit the Tubman attractions mentioned in the itinerary here for that town.

Alternatively, you could get in touch with Blackwater Adventures to see about renting bikes or kayaks for a different way to explore this Tubman countryside.

Tourism info: Dorchester County (Md.) Tourism

BLACKWATER NATIONAL WILDLIFE REFUGE

Sprawling across 20,000 acres below Cambridge, the refuge delivers some of the most breathtaking scenery the Delmarva Peninsula has to offer. The most popular public experience of Blackwater involves driving or pedaling the 3.6-mile-long Wildlife Drive in search of eagles, shorebirds, songbirds, geese, and other avian marvels. There are a couple places to park and take a forested stroll along the way. If you make one run through that drive and come up disappointed—make a second loop. Things can change that quickly out there.

Things change over the long term of centuries, too. While Blackwater has a timeless, unchanging feel, it's actually as good a place as any to get in touch with the forces, both natural and manmade, that have been shaping and reshaping Eastern Shore landscapes for centuries now. As recently as the 1800s, the vast marshland here was mostly productive farmland. That changed because waters here have been rising for centuries, while land has been sinking in a geological phenomenon known as subsidence. One other tidbit: In the early 1900s some entrepreneurial types decided that this would be the perfect place for a fur farm. They imported a hideous-looking but very furry rodent from South America, the nutria, only to go bankrupt in the end. The invasive nutria they left behind would wreak damaging havoc in these marshes for decades before finally (fingers crossed anyway) being eradicated.

The visitor center at Blackwater has some interesting exhibits, a lovely little garden, spotting scopes, a gift shop, and more. For more great scenery, find your way to Maple Dam Road behind the refuge, turn to the south, and make the glorious run out to the Shorter's Wharf boat ramp.

Tourism info: Dorchester County (Md.) Tourism

"Down Below" Itinerary

Most tourists in Dorchester County don't venture beyond the beauty of the Blackwater refuge and the history at the Tubman center, but there is great wandering to be had farther "Down Below," to borrow the term locals often use to describe the remote southern reaches of the county. Here, you can drive to Hoopers Island, which is actually two islands joined by a high, sweeping bridge. Stop at Old Salty's for a classic Eastern Shore dining experience. Back on the mainland, turn south for a scenic run through the rural outposts of Crapo (stop laughing—it's pronounced CRAY-po), Wingate, Bishops Head, and Crocheron. Along the way is the fittingly named World's End Creek.

If you turn north instead, there's another glorious run along Smithville Road en route to Taylors Island, home to a pair of magnificent old churches as well as a cannon that tells the story of an obscure but fascinating World War II battle. If you want to stretch your legs, the Robinson Neck Preserve trail runs for a mile and a quarter or so.

Making your way back to Cambridge along Taylors Island Road, keep an eye out for Old Trinity Episcopal, which dates to the 1600s and ranks as one of the Eastern Shore's oldest churches. Several Revolutionary War veterans are buried in the pretty cemetery.

Tourism info: Dorchester County (Md.) Tourism

CHESAPEAKE COUNTRY MURAL TRAIL

There's plein air painting, and there are plain air paintings. The latter is the focus along the Chesapeake Country Mural Trail of eight outdoor works created by Michael Rosato, a nationally celebrated artist who makes his home here on the Eastern Shore. The trail begins in Cambridge, where five Rosato works explore the natural, cultural, and historical threads of Eastern Shore life. Two other murals are in the nearby towns of Vienna, East New Market, and Hurlock. The best known of these works is "Take My Hand," a trompe l'oeil masterpiece that will leave you feeling like you just reached through the portals of time to touch hands with Underground Railroad conductor (and Eastern Shore native) Harriet Tubman.

Other murals explore the lives of watermen, the ways of Native Americans, and the stories of small-town life. Dorchester County Tourism has a good online guide to the murals. An audio tour via cell phone app is available there, too.

If you want to expand this journey beyond Dorchester, you can find info online about Rosato murals at the Eastern Shore

National Wildlife Refuge near Cape Charles, Va.; in downtown Crisfield, Md.; in Easton, Md.; and on Tilghman Island, Md.
Tourism info: Dorchester County (Md.) Tourism

LOWER HARRIET TUBMAN BYWAY

I have already mentioned the big Tubman Visitors Center out in the Dorchester County countryside and a trio of Tubman attractions in Cambridge, but those are just a small sampling of what this stretch of the Lower Eastern Shore has to offer when it comes to following in the footsteps of Tubman and other, lesser known, heroes of the Underground Railroad.

The rural landscapes to the south and north of Cambridge are chock full of sites of interest—an old canal here, an old church there, an old shipbuilding center up ahead, and a one-room schoolhouse around the next bend. These sites have all been gathered under the umbrella of the Harriet Tubman Underground Railroad Byway, which is organized geographically for your road-tripping convenience. There's an audio guide, too.

If you want to dig a little deeper while on this journey, another option is my book, *Tubman Travels: 32 Underground Railroad Journeys on Delmarva*. It serves up a similar (though not identical) road-tripping itinerary while telling fuller, more in-depth stories about the events that transpired at the various sites and why they matter.

Tourism info: Dorchester County (Md.) Tourism

CHAPTER SEVEN:
LOWER DELAWARE DESTINATIONS

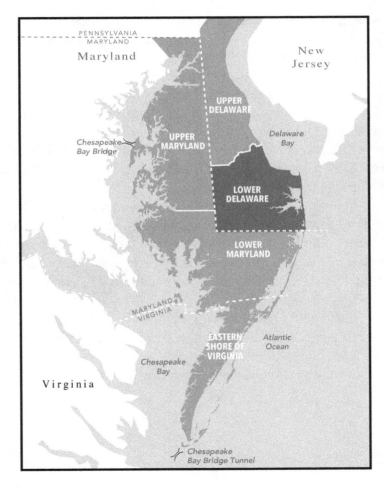

FENWICK ISLAND ITINERARY

The trick to approaching Fenwick Island Lighthouse lies in managing expectations. If you arrive with your heart set on finding a beacon standing in scenic, stately fashion on an isolated stretch of coastline, you will be disappointed. This conical brick lighthouse rises to its height of 87 feet from the midst of a crowded stretch of 146th Street full of trailers, homes, and businesses.

That backdrop, however, puts the history of this stretch of coastline in perspective. Nothing was here when the lighthouse went up in 1859. The only way to get to Fenwick then was by boat. The fuel used in its original light was whale oil. The first smidgeons of development came in the early 1900s, but that process didn't go into overdrive until Coastal Highway was built in the 1950s. As of this writing, the lighthouse is staffed by volunteers only a few hours a week, and visitors are not allowed to climb up into the tower, so plan accordingly.

Fenwick Island State Park offers three miles of sandy bliss. For old-school country shopping, stop at the Seaside Country Market. The Fenwick Boardwalk serves up junk food joy. Lots of mini-golf and other family-friendly diversions nearby. Don't miss the DiscoverSea Shipwreck Museum—it's listed separately here.

Last but not least: As you might have heard, Fenwick Island has a big, beautiful stretch of beach—that's managed as Fenwick Island State Park.

Tourism info: Southern Delaware Tourism

ASSAWOMAN WILDLIFE AREA

Some people thrive on beach-resort crowds; others want to escape them. If you're with me in the latter category, make your way to the Assawoman Wildlife Area, which covers 3,000 acres on Little Assawoman Bay and serves up quiet scenes of pine woods, marshland beauty, and waterfront vistas. At times you'll see the Ocean City high-rises, but it'll still feel like you're a world away. A driving-tour brochure should be available near the park entrance. Be sure to stop and climb the observation tower overlooking Mulberry Pond. If you're in paddling mode, look up the Sassafras Landing Water Trail.

The obvious question about the strange, giggle-inducing name of the two inland bays here—one "Big" and one "Little"—remains a bit of a mystery. You will find some talk on the internet about how Assawoman refers to female members of an Indian tribe, but most folks with expertise in Native American matters seem to think that we simply don't know what this word meant to folks who spoke the old Algonquian languages.

Tourism info: Southern Delaware Tourism

DISCOVERSEA SHIPWRECK MUSEUM

Most museums on the Delmarva Peninsula fall into one of two categories, a traditional nonprofit or a government-run facility. DiscoverSea Shipwreck Museum in Fenwick Island is different—it's a privately run labor of love put together by the diver, treasure hunter, and amateur archaeologist Dale W. Clifton Jr. Clifton caught the shipwreck bug as a boy after hearing talk about a stretch of sand near the Indian River Inlet some folks called

"Coin Beach."

He spent most of a year combing through the sand there on a regular basis before he finally found a piece of what he was looking for. He started thinking about the fact that no human being had touched that coin for 200 years. And then he started wondering who back then might have been the last person to touch it before him. "It was like shaking hands with history," he recalls.

That is kind of the mission statement for his museum, as that moment set him off on a long career of hunting for shipwrecks near and far. Housed on the second floor of a retail building, it might look a bit dicey on the attractiveness scale from the outside. Inside, however, it's quite a beautiful showcase for what may rank as the largest private collection of shipwreck artifacts in the country. On display are coins, weapons, china, keys, gold bars, and much more.

Tourism info: Southern Delaware Tourism

BETHANY BEACH ITINERARY

As with the other beach resorts here, there is no rocket science involved in visiting Bethany Beach. You stroll the main drag. You wander the boardwalk. You enjoy the beach. Once a year on a midsummer evening, I do a book signing while set up at a table outside of Bethany Beach Books. During those evenings, I have come to this conclusion: There might be no happier place on earth than the post-dinner hours when throngs of people are eating ice cream cones while walking up and down Garfield Boulevard.

The town is full of great backstories, from its genesis as a remote religious retreat through the various and fascinating transportation improvements that helped transform it into a resort and right on up to the present day. Those stories are well told on exhibit panels and through artifacts housed on the main floor of City Hall as well as in the new Dinker-Irvin House museum that's just across the highway on Garfield Boulevard.

The kids or grandkids will enjoy the Bethany Beach Nature Center. Take a self-guided hike along the Fresh Pond Trail. Stroll or pedal along the banks of the Assawoman Canal. As of this writing there were two fun wild kingdom options farther out in that countryside—the Barn Hill Preserve (sloths! otters!) and Goat Joy (yes, goats!).

When you get back into town, don't forget about that ice cream cone after dinner.

Tourism info: Southern Delaware Tourism

JAMES FARM ECOLOGICAL PRESERVE AND HOLTS LANDING STATE PARK

If you find yourself in need of a little peace and quiet during your busy beach-resort adventures, these two parks will deliver the serenity you need. The 150-acre James Farm Ecological Preserve on the southern shore of Indian River Bay is managed by the nonprofit Delaware Center for Inland Bays and offers three miles of trails, three observation decks, wildflower gardens, and sweet waterfront views. Along the way you can explore seven distinct natural habitats, from low saltmarsh up to lush meadows and maritime forests. Be sure to take the trail out to the beach, as that spot overlooking Pasture Point Cove is gorgeous.

The 200-acre Holts Landing State Park has been dubbed by one newspaper reporter as "Delaware's unknown park." It has a little beach on the bay, along with stretches of hardwood forests for hiking. There's a playground for the kids. It's home to the only pier on the Delaware bays built specifically for crabbing. Take the Sea Hawk Trail as it meanders for one and a quarter miles through various habitats—hardwood forest, meadow, salt-marsh, and freshwater bog.

Tourism info: Southern Delaware Tourism

DELAWARE SEASHORE STATE PARK

With six miles of oceanfront and 20 miles of inland bay shore-line, the 2,800-acre Delaware Seashore State Park is a haven for sunbathers, anglers, hikers, paddlers, boaters, and more. The thin stretch of land here used to be an ever-changing affair. One storm would blow open an inlet linking the ocean and the inland bays. Another one would close it. A third would open an inlet in a new spot. And so it went, until stabilizing jetties were built in the late 1930s.

In addition to those long stretches of beach and shoreline, you can follow a trail out to Burton Island, exploring a stretch of saltmarsh ecosystem that's as pretty as it is pristine. Those marsh-es offer rich habitats for resident and migrating birds, so bring your camera. Alas, no remnants remain of the old hunting clubs that stood out here at the turn of the 20th century, when rich New Yorkers and Philadelphians came down in droves to get their fill of hunting, fishing, and drinking. (Fair warning: It's best to take this excursion in the tick-free cooler months.)

In the warmer months, you'll be able to enjoy breath-taking ocean views from the deck at the Big Chill Beach Club, located right inside the park. And don't forget to visit the Indian River Life-Saving Station, listed separately here.

Tourism info: Southern Delaware Tourism

INDIAN RIVER LIFE-SAVING STATION

The legendary "surfmen" who toiled at the Indian River Life-Saving Station responded to more than 60 wrecks and saved more than 400 lives in the late 1800s and early 1900s. Along with their compatriots up and down the East Coast, they were lionized in the national press as heroic "storm warriors" in the same manner that we honor first responders today.

Located between Dewey Beach and Bethany Beach, the station was built in 1876. It got mostly buried in sand during a ferocious storm in the 1960s, but it is now restored to the way it looked in 1905. What I like about the place is its engaging simplicity. You will not find much in the way of bells and whistles (though the cell phone tour is well done). Instead, you will walk through a bunk room, a dining area, and a pantry that communicate quite genuinely how spartan a lifestyle those "surfmen" of yore endured.

Several times a year in the summertime Indian River conducts re-creations of old-school "breeches buoy" style rescues using a method that resembles a modern-day zip line. Surfmen would use cannon-like "Lyle" guns to shoot lines equipped with leg harnesses and pulleys as far as 600 yards. In past years the station has also put on special dinner events featuring the sorts of simple, local foods that surfmen might have enjoyed.

Tourism info: Southern Delaware Tourism

Rehoboth Beach Itinerary

It's not exactly rocket science here. You stroll the boardwalk. You chill out on the sandy beach. You wander the shops. You eat in style in the foodiest of Delmarva's beach resorts.

The best place to get acclimated to the stories of the place is the Rehoboth Beach Museum, which isn't one of those musty outfits where you get deluged with details about matters that seem trivial to anyone other than hardcore local history buffs. Here, the backstories of this famous resort town come into focus in a fashion that's quick, engaging, and professional. You'll see Rehoboth taking root by way of lifesaving "surfmen" and religious camp meetings. You'll learn how the place came into full flower as a resort thanks in no small part to its popularity with artists and the gay community. You'll smile over the vintage bathing suits, beach toys, and old postcards. You might want to check in advance to see if one of their walking or trolley tours is available.

Another stop thick with history is the Rehoboth Art League. Founded in 1938, the league is set on a gorgeous campus where you can see not just exhibits of works by its 1,000-plus members but also the 1743 Peter Marsh Homestead and its glorious Homestead Garden. If you are more into modern-day consumer joys, there are outlet malls galore along the highway.

Tourism info: Southern Delaware Tourism

Cape Henlopen State Park

The 5,000-acre Cape Henlopen State Park didn't take official shape until 1964, but the story of its status as open-to-the-public property dates to the days of William Penn. Back in 1682 when Delaware was still a part of Pennsylvania, a man named Edmond

Warner asked Penn for permission to set up a "coney," or rabbit warren, on the cape. Penn said yes, but in doing so he specified in writing that the non-rabbit glories of the Cape—its berries, marshland, fishing grounds, timberlands, etc.—should be "reserved for public use." The language of that "Warner Grant" is arguably the first time anyone in what would become the United States formalized the notion of setting aside something like a big piece of parkland.

The most popular attraction at Cape Henlopen today is a long stretch of beach, but you will also find hiking trails, a fishing pier, and the Seaside Nature Center. The remains of World War II-era Fort Miles are here, too, so you will be able to check out underground gun batteries, see old military buildings, and photograph castle-like observation towers that served as lookout stations for foreign invaders.

Be sure to make your way to the stretch of beach where the Delaware Breakwater East End Light stands a little way offshore. That iconic beacon was built in 1885.

Tourism info: Southern Delaware Tourism

TAKE A HIKE IN REHOBOTH AND LEWES

Some of the best strolling options in the Lewes and Rehoboth Beach areas are obvious. Walk the boardwalk in Rehoboth. Meander along one beach or another. Stroll Canalfront Park in Lewes.

The Junction and Breakwater Trail follows an old railroad line that ran between the two towns, delivering tourists from the big city in the early years of the 20th century. Fit for cycling, walking, and jogging, it runs nearly six miles one way. There's also a short-but-sweet path (just a quarter mile or so) that meanders along the shores of pretty Lake Gerar in Rehoboth.

My photographer wife has a clear favorite here. Gordons Pond Trail awaits on the southern end of Cape Henlopen State Park. She insists on walking that trail every time we're in the area, and it takes us roughly forever to do that, as she's constantly stopping and shooting this gaggle of birds, that stretch of waterfront, that stand of trees, this little turtle, or that little rabbit. Along the way are historic markers, elevated overlooks, and views of World War II-era observation towers. My wife is right (as always)—it's gorgeous out there.

Tourism info: Southern Delaware Tourism

ZWAANENDAEL MUSEUM

The skinny, steeply tiered home of the Zwaanendael Museum will look familiar if you happen to hail from Hoorn, as its design is based on the city hall in that Dutch town. The museum was built in 1931 to celebrate the 300th anniversary of the arrival of Dutch settlers under the command of Peter de Vries—that's a statue of him up on the roof.

The exhibits inside tell the story of Lewes from that ill-fated Dutch outpost through its growth as a seafaring town in the 1800s and up to its transformation into a tourism destination. One fascinating focus is on the *DeBraak*, a British warship that arrived off the Delaware coast on May 25, 1798, only to go down in a storm that took the lives of its cantankerous captain and 45 other sailors. If you can, sign up for one of the museum's frequent presentations on the *DeBraak*—it might include a chance to go see the ship's old hull, which is stored nearby.

Saving the best for last: Zwaanendael is home to the oddest, ugliest object in Lewes, a "Fiji Merman." Seen lounging in a display case on a velvet cushion, the wannabe mermaid is actually a hideous looking thing, the head of a dead monkey attached to the body of a fish. Making such ugly (to our eyes) creatures was something of a folk art in Japan and the East Indies in the 1800s—it was tied to religious practices somehow.

A ship captain brought one back to America, and it ended up in the hands of the famed circus entrepreneur P.T. Barnum, who (with help from fake experts) turned it into proof that mermaids were real. That merman caused quite the national sensation. The one here is not the Barnum original, but a different "merman" that ended up in the hands of a local family, the Martins. They loaned it to Zwaanendael in 1941, and it's been entertaining and horrifying visitors ever since.

Tourism info: Southern Delaware Tourism

LEWES ITINERARY

Known as the "First Town" in the "First State," Lewes stands today near where Dutch settlers erected a fort in 1631. That settlement didn't last, but its successor city is still thriving. Even a century ago, one writer was marveling over how Lewes was the "saltiest" town in the state, blessed with traditions "of the sea borne by every east wind that haunts its narrow streets and aged cypress-shingled houses. ... [It] is to Delaware what Plymouth is to Massachusetts and Jamestown is to Virginia."

Stroll the few short blocks of downtown, browsing through shops here and grabbing a meal. Along the way you'll find the Gothic-style St. Peter's Episcopal Church. The oldest stone in the graveyard there belongs to a woman born in 1631. Meander over to Canalfront Park for a stroll through those salty maritime centuries. You can tour the Lightship Overfalls there—

it's a rare survivor among the nearly 200 floating lighthouses built by the U.S. government between 1820 and 1952. The park also has an old boathouse, a restored Monomoy lifeboat, and a run of historic markers detailing tales from Lewes days gone by. The 1812 Memorial Park is nearby. There, you can learn about the wild War of 1812 days when Lewes got bombed by the Brits.

The Lewes Historical Society is one of the most active and successful outfits of its kind in the region. The society's lineup includes a country store, a ferry house, a doctor's office, a one-room school, and more. The Lewes History Museum on Adams Avenue is a society project as well—the exhibit materials there are first-rate. Check in advance on the society's always busy schedule of events, walking tours, and history-by-boat excursions.

Did I mention that there's a beach in Lewes? Or that you can drive aboard the Cape May-Lewes Ferry and sail across the bay to New Jersey?

Tourism info: Southern Delaware Tourism

PRIME HOOK NATIONAL WILDLIFE REFUGE

This 10,000-acre swath of natural goodness awaits just a few miles north of Lewes. Prime Hook became a refuge in the 1960s, but its name dates to the 1600s when the Dutch settled in this area. The Dutch words *priume hoek* translate as "Plum Point" a reference to the beach plums that grow here.

You can see exhibit materials and pepper volunteer docents with questions at the visitor center. Explore the park by driving along one of four roads running through marshland or walking some or all of seven miles of trails. Step up on an observation deck in search of birds. Enjoy fishing, paddling, and hunt-

214

ing. Plus, a big stretch of beach.

The scenes that unfold at Prime Hook will seem timeless and pristine, but the place has actually been through a world of transition lately. Starting with Hurricane Ernesto in 2006 and running through Hurricane Sandy in 2012, one storm after another battered Prime Hook, opening up breaches that sent saltwater pouring inland and drowning the freshwater marshes. Starting in 2015, refuge officials spent nearly $40 million and four years to restore beaches and reestablish the freshwater marshes. One aspect of that project—the restoration of Fowler Beach—was ranked by the American Shore and Beach Preservation Association among the five best projects of its kind in the country.

Tourism info: Southern Delaware Tourism

THE UNCROWDED BEACHES

Most folks heading to the Delaware beaches make a beeline along the Route 1 highway until they reach one or another of the famous resort towns: Lewes, Rehoboth, Dewey, Bethany, and Fenwick Island. But if you get off that highway and travel the pretty backroads that head east, you'll find one lesser known stretch of sand after another.

There will be no boardwalks, no taffy, and no fries. But there won't be any big crowds, either, as you go about the business of strolling, beachcombing, and castle building. There are more of these beaches here than you could hit in a single day, although hey, you could try! Starting from Lewes on the south, there is Broadkill Beach, then Prime Hook Beach, then Fowler Beach, then Slaughter Beach, then Big Stone Beach, then Bennett's Pier Beach.

Stores and restaurants will be few and far between, though

the little store at Broadkill Beach is great touristy fun. One other idea: If you make your way south from Broadkill, you'll be able to park and then set off on a long, sandy walk down to and through the Beach Plum Island Nature Preserve.

One easy way to find these beaches is to set your favorite map software in Lewes and just scroll north. Searching the internet for the various beach names here will work, too.

Tourism info: Southern Delaware Tourism

THE DUPONT NATURE CENTER AT SLAUGHTER BEACH

There is one more beach to explore in the upper reaches of Sussex County—Slaughter Beach, and this one has an added attraction. Open during the warmer months, the DuPont Nature Center stands out on a peninsula overlooking the pretty Mispillion Harbor, where two waterways, the Mispillion River and Cedar Creek, flow out into Delaware Bay. This is where to go for an engaging introduction to the natural history and ecology of this coastline.

The exhibits inside explain why the mixing of saltwater and freshwater here is such a powerful wildlife draw. More than 130 different species frequent the area, from fish and shellfish to resident and migrating birds. You'll learn, too, about the role that our beautiful saltmarshes play in serving as a buffer against pollution and erosion. The most famous of the creatures here is actually a sea spider, though everyone calls it the horseshoe crab. These prehistoric marvels—the Delaware Bay has the biggest population of horseshoes in the world—clamber up out of the water each spring in a spawning ritual that ranks among the greatest of Delmarva's many natural wonders. You can learn at the Nature Center how to plan an excursion during May or June to try to watch that unfold.

With a prime location and some powerful spotting scopes, the deck at DuPont is regarded by birders as an excellent place to watch migrating birds in the spring. That deck is open and accessible even when the center is closed during fall and winter, so this is a great place to admire the array of shorebirds that stop here during those seasons—dunlins, sanderlings, and black-bellied plovers among them. The center also has excellent hands-on activities for kids.

Tourism info: Southern Delaware Tourism

DELAWARE BOTANIC GARDENS AT PEPPER CREEK

If you have not heard of Piet Oudolf, join the club. I was in that position before visiting the newish Delaware Botanic Gardens at Pepper Creek. This 37-acre tract located on the backroads outside of Dagsboro, Del. opened in 2019 after a decade's worth of planting and preparation. Much of that work happened under the guidance of Oudolf, a Dutchman whose name is instantly recognizable to landscape design nerds.

Consider this from Gardenista, a website regarded by some as the bible of gardening: "If the world of gardening has rock stars, Piet Oudolf qualifies as Mick Jagger, David Bowie, and Prince rolled into one." Oudolf's work falls into a genre known as "New Perennial," in which pretty flowers stand not on their own, but amid swatches of tall, swaying grasses that serve as a natural version of the sort of dreamily romantic background you might find in Impressionist paintings. The trick here has been compared to setting a mood, "like candlelight at a dinner party."

The five gardens at Pepper Creek are mere toddlers as of

this writing. They will continue to grow and evolve through the 2020s, after which the landscape is expected to achieve a fuller measure of the maturity envisioned by its famed designer. The folks who hired Oudolf to work here are not at all shy about saying the goal here is a "world-class" facility. One last bit of advice: No matter how entranced you get by the the flowers, don't skip out on the forest paths and their waterfront views.

Another Dagsboro tip: Wander the grounds of Prince George's Chapel—it dates to the 1750s.

Tourism info: Southern Delaware Tourism

RIDIN' THE LINE ON ROUTE 54

When I drive across Delaware from my home in Maryland on the way to one beach town or another I try sometimes to take different two-lane roads through the rural countryside. One of my favorites is Route 54, which spends much of its length in southernmost Delaware straddling the border with Maryland—a line that was the subject of much contention back in colonial times.

There will not be much in the way of tourist attractions and creature comforts, but there will be a lot of glorious scenery and interesting little towns. I will start on the east here, though you might just as easily start on the west. Pick up Route 54 at Fenwick Island—initially, the route will be full of new housing developments, but those will fade away the closer you get to Selbyville, which dates its history from 1778. There is a fun legend about the town's name—supposedly, an enterprising country store owner named Sampson Selby rather randomly started telling people to address deliveries to him at "Selby-ville." Darned if the postal service didn't go along. The town's heyday came in the late 1800s and early 1900s when it was a leading player in the big strawberry boom that erupted once the railroad arrived.

Follow Route 54 through a few turns on the way to itty-bitty Gumboro. That town stands roughly halfway between the ocean and Maryland. There is some chatter online about a haunted house here. If that makes you curious, search the internet for info about "The Old Homestead in Gumboro."

Route 54 becomes Line Road after that and quite literally straddles the border. It's a pretty ride, leading through farm fields here and horse farms there. Keep an eye out for Line Church if you want to stretch your legs by wandering a pretty cemetery. You'll cross the Route 13 highway at Delmar, whose slogan is "the little town too big for one state."

Route 54 becomes Delmar Road there. After about eight miles stop at the blink-and-you'll-miss-it little pull-off on the north. Most of us learned about the Mason-Dixon Line as a big deal during the lead-up to the Civil War, because it separated free states in the North from the slave states in the South. When that line was first "drawn" in the 1760s, however, it had nothing to do with slavery. It was designed to end a longstanding boundary fight between the colonies of Maryland and Pennsylvania (which then included the "Lower Counties" of Delaware).

Surveyors Charles Mason and Jeremiah Dixon put in their share of time here on the Delmarva Peninsula. The stone marker that stands here behind some iron grating is a vestige of that undertaking—it was, in fact, their starting point in ending that border dispute. After a few more miles, well, welcome to Maryland.

TIP JAR: If you haven't seen enough small towns yet, maybe make a run up to pretty Sharptown, Md. and/or make an advance appointment to see the Adkins Historical & Museum Complex and the Barren Creek Village in Mardela Springs, Md.

Tourism info: Southern Delaware Tourism

BETHEL, LAUREL, AND THE WOODLAND FERRY

The Woodland Ferry dates its history as a Nanticoke River crossing clear back to the 1740s, which means that even the mildest of history buffs will want to make their way southwest of Seaford to drive aboard and take that short ride. If you had taken that ride in 1793, it would have cost five cents per person or horse and 10 cents for a carriage. If you'd made that ride in 1843, you might have witnessed the notorious murder of ferry owner Jacob Cannon Jr.

Once you land back on asphalt, find your way into Bethel, a small town on Broad Creek where mighty big ships were built back in the day. Grab a sandwich at the throwback Bethel Store, stroll through streets full of houses built by sea captains of yore, and/or find your way to one or both of Bethel's historic graveyards. One good time to make this trip is on first Sundays in the warmer months, as the Bethel Historical Society should be open.

That opening happens in coordination with several sites in nearby Laurel, another town thick with history. Once the wealthiest town in Delaware, Laurel's historic district is chock full of Queen Anne Revival, Victorian Gothic, and Colonial Revival gems. The First Sunday openings here include the Laurel Historical Society, where you can learn about the canneries and basketmaking factories that once flourished along Broad Creek. Don't skip out on the chance to see Old Christ Church, as that 40-foot-by-60-foot wooden church dates to 1772 and stands as a remarkable remnant from colonial times.

Tourism info: Southern Delaware Tourism

TRAP POND STATE PARK

Much of inland Sussex County used to be part of the vast and spooky Great Cypress Swamp, which covered 50,000 acres here and across the border in Maryland. Remnants of that swamp survive just outside the town of Laurel at Trap Pond State Park, which has 12 miles of water trails in addition to hiking paths and a Baldcypress Nature Center. Last I checked, the park offered free bicycles and rental kayaks and pedal boats. Plus, horseshoe pits, a disc golf course, and a playground. A busy events calendar includes alfresco concerts, hayrides, nighttime lantern tours, and pontoon excursions.

The swamps of yore were so thick that they never really saw the full light of day—it was always somewhere between dark and semi-dark—"one of the most frightful labyrinths you can imagine," in the words of a traveler in 1809. It should come as no surprise, then, that the swamp served as a popular hiding place over the centuries for everyone from British loyalists and runaway slaves to moonshiners and criminals on the run.

Tourism info: Southern Delaware Tourism

NANTICOKE INDIAN MUSEUM

The only museum in Delaware devoted to Native American history stands in the countryside west of Millville, along Route 24. Housed in a former school attended by local Indian children, the Nanticoke Indian Museum tells the story of a tribe whose name translates as the "tidewater people."

The facility looks quite small from the outside, but it is jam-packed inside with artifacts and displays. You'll get to see a dugout canoe, traditional clothing, and lots of artwork. You'll see headdresses, jewelry, pottery, spears, arrowheads, and baskets—including a tiny one made of peach pits.

Along the way you'll pick up the thread of the larger Nanticoke journey. Before Europeans arrived, they sustained themselves through fishing, trapping, and gathering. They went to war to protect their lands in the 1640s. They were relegated to reservation life during the 1690s. Many Nanticokes gave up on Delaware in the early 1700s, migrating north to join up with the then-powerful Iroquois Nation. From there, a remnant would move west and join up with another tribe that used to make its home in this area, the Delaware.

A few Nanticoke chose to stay put and blend in with the local population. It's their descendants who formed the nonprofit Nanticoke Indian Association that runs this museum. One of those local Indians will probably be on hand to guide you through the collection or answer questions.

Tourism info: Southern Delaware Tourism

SEAFORD ITINERARY

Seaford's best-known tourism attraction is the Gov. Ross Plantation, which occupies 20 of the 1,400 acres that once belonged to William Henry Harrison Ross around the time of the Civil War. As a young man, Ross played around with the then-newfangled idea of growing peach trees, an experiment that soon bore voluminous fruit, covering more than 800 acres of his plantation. Elected governor of Delaware in 1851 at the age of 36, Ross still ranks as the youngest man ever elected to that post.

Today, the Gov. Ross Plantation ranks among the best places in Delaware to get a full sense for life in plantation times. The centerpiece of the property is a three-story Italianate mansion that dates to the 1850s. Sign on for a tour of the interior to see lots of period furnishings and art. A slave owner, Ross became an ardent supporter of the South and its "peculiar institution" in his later years. The grounds boast several interesting outbuildings, including a rare surviving slave quarter.

Find your way from there into downtown Seaford, home to the little Nanticoke Riverwalk. As you walk uphill from there into the heart of downtown, you'll be walking in the footsteps of Harriet Tubman, who led an escaping slave named Tilly along that same route. You'll pass shops and restaurants on your way to the interesting and idiosyncratic Seaford Museum, run by the local historical society out of an old post office building.

If you're in the mood for a walk through the woods, head southwest of town to find the Chapel Branch Nature Trail. A little farther south beyond that are two more strolling options, the Barnes Wood Nature Preserve and Woodland Park.

Tourism info: Southern Delaware Tourism

GEORGETOWN ITINERARY

The seat of Sussex County boasts one of the prettiest town squares on Delmarva, though in this case it's a circle—a traffic circle bounded by a run of historic buildings. To get the lay of the land, check the hours or make an appointment at the interesting Marvel Carriage Museum. In addition to a swell collection of antique carriages and local-history photos and artifacts, the museum grounds include historic Delaware buildings moved from other sites, including a one-room schoolhouse, a blacksmith shop, and two railroad stations. Ask about the Western Auto Museum, too— that's a tribute to a famous chain store from days gone by.

Just off of that scenic circle, downtown Georgetown has a

modest collection of shops and eateries. The town is a hub for the local Latino community, so you'll have various Hispanic cuisines to choose from. The little airport here is home to the appointment-only Delaware Aviation Museum, which boasts a collection of vintage aircraft and aviation memorabilia.

Get in touch with a centuries-old shipwreck tale by going to see "Treasures of the Sea" in the Stephen J. Betze Library at Delaware Technical Community College. The exhibit details the sad fate of the Spanish galleon *Nuestra Señora de Atocha* and its sister ship, *Santa Margarita*. Both went down off the coast of Florida amid wicked winds and high waves during a 1622 storm. For more than three centuries afterward, treasure hunters went looking for the gold, silver, and jewels that were reportedly aboard. With financial backing from Georgetown businessman Melvin Joseph, treasure hunter Mel Fisher located the wrecks in the 1980s, recovering more than 1,000 silver bars, 180,000 silver coins, and several bronze cannons. Visitors to this exhibit can watch a short film about the wreck and its aftermath, then see some of the recovered artifacts that became Joseph's share of the booty.

For a touch of nature, find your way north of town to the Redden State Forest.

Tourism info: Southern Delaware Tourism

MILTON ITINERARY

If your Delaware travel routine has you constantly locked onto highways, it's high time you mixed things up. Milton is a fine excuse to do just that. A shipbuilding town on the Broadkill River, it's full of old homes from Victorian and colonial times. Browse the adorable little downtown, then stroll along the river in pretty

Memorial Park.

Stop in at the Milton Historical Society to get a feel for the place. When they do their occasional walking tours, they dub the experience "Boats, Buttons, Beans, and Beer." Whether you take that tour or just wander the museum, you'll learn about the countless stories Milton has to tell about shipbuilding, button factories, and canneries. That beer business is because the tour starts and ends at the famous Dogfish Head Craft Brewery. You can tour that operation pretty much every day. Take time at the museum to get in the Christmas spirit, too—Milton was once known far and wide as "The Land of Holly" for its work as a supplier of holiday décor.

If a walk through the woods sounds good, find your way to McCabe Preserve just outside of town. If you want to stay into the evening, see what's up at the always interesting Milton Theatre.

Tourism info: Southern Delaware Tourism

MILFORD ITINERARY

The main thing here is to stroll the pretty Riverwalk as it follows the winding Mispillion River through a thriving historic downtown and then into nearby neighborhoods. Milford prides itself on having an artsy vibe, so plan on a little gallery hopping on top of the shopping and dining. There will be signage up along the way to help you learn as you go about a town that got its name from a water-powered sawmill that was up and running in the 1600s.

You can dig deeper into the town's stories at the Milford Museum, which shines a spotlight on the array of colorful characters who've laid their hats here over the centuries. One example: Back in the early 1900s, a lifelong wanderer named John Mulholland settled here and decided that he could make ice cream taste better. He succeeded, too. You'll learn, too, how the town really came into its own as a shipbuilding center in the 1800s. Civic leaders have been working hard in recent years to preserve the last of those old shipyards and turn it into a cultural and tourism asset for the town.

Tourism info: Southern Delaware Tourism and/or Kent County (Del.) Tourism

ABBOTT'S MILL

Located a few miles southwest of Milford, Abbott's Mill is a survivor from the days when farmers depended on local gristmills to process their wheat and corn. Town after town after town on Delmarva had mills like this, but survivors from those days are few and far between.

A water-powered mill has been up and running on this site for 150-plus years, from the presidency of James Madison through the year of John F. Kennedy's election. The two-and-a-half story mill building that stands along a bend in Abbotts Pond Road—it was probably built on the foundation of an earlier mill—is in great shape for its age, as you will see while wandering its nooks and crannies and admiring the various nearby outbuildings. In recent years, they've powered the mill up on the third Saturdays of warmer months.

There is much more than the mill to see. The site covers nearly 400 acres. Hiking trails wind through forests and meadows and along the shores of a 20-acre millpond. The nature center is a little museum, with exhibits about wildlife.

Tourism info: Southern Delaware Tourism and/or Kent County (Del.) Tourism

CHAPTER EIGHT:
UPPER DELAWARE DESTINATIONS

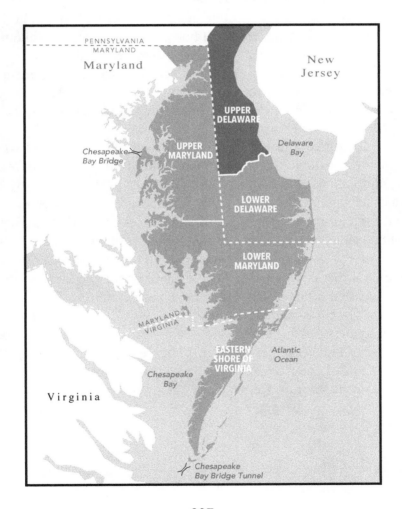

BOWERS BEACH

Appropriately enough, the road to Bowers Beach involves leaving the Route 1 Highway at Little Heaven, then wandering eastward along a heavenly backroad. Your destination is an old-time fishing village that dates to the 1600s and stands at the mouth of a river with one of the all-time great names, the Murderkill. If you go looking on the Internet, you will find your way to legends about how this name refers to a big Indian massacre, but the truth is more mundane. In Dutch, *moeder* means mother, and *kille* means riverbed. The "Mother River" got named when Dutch settlers ruled the roost here. Later, English colonists butchered both the pronunciation and the spelling.

Bring your beach gear, as you will have a choice of two sandy destinations. The busier one is near the center of town on the north side of the river, and it's got lots of safe and shallow water for younger kids. The other, lesser traveled one is on the south side of the river. The Murderkill is a skinny little thing here, but no bridge crosses it so getting to those southern sands is going to involve a 20-minute ride back out to the highway and around again. Farther down on that side of the river are two more road-less-traveled beaches, Big Stone Beach and Bennett's Pier.

The town is great for strolling or pedaling around, as it has a timeless vibe. The Bowers Beach Maritime Museum is open weekends in the warmer months. A couple of eateries were up and running last I checked. Fishing charters are available, too.

Tourism info: Kent County (Del.) Tourism

BARRATT'S CHAPEL AND MUSEUM

A pair of famous "Great Awakenings" swept like mass fevers through Delmarva, first before and then after the Revolutionary War. At Barratt's Chapel and Museum, you can get a sense for the way those cultural revolutions transformed the lives of common folks in small towns all over the peninsula.

This 1780 chapel off of Route 1 near Frederica was ground zero for the second of those Great Awakenings. A lot of Methodist ministers fled back to England when the Revolution began, but Rev. Francis Asbury and a cadre of other devoted believers set up shop here and set about spreading their Good News as "circuit riders," riding horses and wagons to preaching engagements throughout the countryside.

In the estimation of one University of Delaware historian, what they accomplished makes Barratt's Chapel "the most important Methodist historical structure in the nation" and "the most significant historical building, secular or religious, on the entire Delmarva Peninsula." The chapel is home to a museum and a library nowadays. Tours are available a couple of days a week as of this writing. On display there are old handwritten sermons and journals, along with lots of fascinating memorabilia.

Tourism info: Kent County (Del.) Tourism

HARRINGTON AND KILLENS POND

It will be hard to imagine while rolling through the agricultural heartland around Harrington, but this land was all woods when

Europeans first arrived. The place has its roots in a 1780s tavern that opened in that forestland and served as a stagecoach stop. A full-fledged town took shape once the railroad arrived in the 1850s. Canneries, shirt factories, and other industries popped up soon after. You can explore those transformations in a trio of sites maintained by the Harrington Historical Society—a little museum, an old church, and a railroad tower, though they are only open once a month or so. Find your way to the John Deere tractor dealer Taylor & Messick to see their little Messick Agricultural Museum.

The town is most famous nowadays as the site of the humongous Delaware State Fair every July and the home of the Harrington Raceway & Casino, so you might want to pack along a good-luck charm or two. Also, there is ice skating at the Centre Ice Arena during fall, winter, and spring.

Just north of Harrington, Killens Pond State Park is centered on a 66-acre manmade millpond that dates to the 1700s. You can go for a shoreline hike, rent kayaks or canoes, or visit a little nature center. If you have kids or grandkids in tow, they will go gaga for the water park, with its giant swirling slides and spouting water jets.

Tourism info: Kent County (Del.) Tourism

JOHN DICKINSON PLANTATION

When Quaker tobacco farmer Samuel Dickinson moved from Talbot County, Md. to land southeast of Dover in 1740, he and his wife had a seven-year-old boy in tow who had his heart set on making an "immense bustle in the world." John Dickinson would do just that, becoming a prominent lawyer, a successful plantation farmer, and a patriot.

In the 1760s, he earned the nickname "Penman of the Revolution" by writing a string of "Letters from a Farmer" arguing that various British taxes were unjust. He had a gift for taking high-falutin' philosophical ideas and presenting them in clear words that regular folks could get behind.

Your visit to his old stomping grounds will be a mix of seeing exhibits, touring the house, and wandering the grounds. The plantation's colonial-style gardens were designed by Alden Hopkins, who also designed some gardens at Colonial Williamsburg. In recent years, the plantation has added an emphasis on the story of slavery, as Dickinson was a slaveholder at the same time he was arguing that white colonists deserved more freedom. To his credit, Dickinson eventually followed the trajectory of many of his Quaker brethren, freeing those slaves in the 1770s and 1780s.

If you want stroll a sandy beach afterward, follow Kitts Hummock Road until it ends.

Tourism info: Kent County (Del.) Tourism

AIR MOBILITY COMMAND MUSEUM

Don't be put off by the bulky name or assume that a museum dedicated to military supply-chain logistics will appeal only to aviation nerds. At this idiosyncratic destination near the Dover Air Force Base, you'll bounce from one cool story to another to the one after that. In an exhibit dedicated to the 1949 Berlin Airlift, there is the tale of Lt. Gail Halvorsen, whose method of delivering treats for the children of Berlin earned him the nickname, "The Candy Bomber." Over in the section on air refueling, there is the story of wing-walking daredevil Wesley May, who on Nov.

21, 1921 strolled out on the wing of one airplane and then crossed over to the wing of another with a five-gallon jug of gas strapped to his back. Yes, both planes were flying. It was the first-ever in-flight refueling success in the history of aviation. The tales keep on coming after that.

The airpark outside is full of cool old planes, including a C-5 Galaxy, the biggest and baddest cargo plane in the history of the world. It stands six stories tall. If it were turned up on its back end, it would rise up to 24 stories. From wingtip to wingtip, it is wider than the White House. Once a month, the museum runs an Open Cockpit Day where you can climb inside many of these old classics.

Tourism info: Kent County (Del.) Tourism

JOHNSON VICTROLA MUSEUM

When Eldridge Reeves Johnson graduated from Dover Academy in 1882, the school's director gave him some blunt advice: "You are too god damned dumb to go to college. Go and learn a trade." He went to work in a machine shop, but then transformed himself into an entrepreneur history regards as "the Steve Jobs of his era."

His journey is the focus of a wonderfully idiosyncratic museum on the edge of downtown Dover, the Johnson Victrola Museum. Over the course of several decades in the early 20th century, Johnson developed the Victor Talking Machine, an early record player that revolutionized the American music industry and made Johnson a millionaire many times over.

You can visit his old office and admire an outstanding collection of Victrolas. Your tour guide will probably play a couple of cool old songs while leading the way through exhibits on two floors. Trivia: Who knew that the phrase "put a sock in it" came from people trying to modulate the volume on their Victrola by, quite literally, stuffing a sock inside the horn?

Tourism info: Kent County (Del.) Tourism

DELAWARE AGRICULTURAL MUSEUM

Take a deep dive into farming traditions at the Delaware Agricultural Museum and Village on the north side of Dover. The grounds are dotted with interesting old buildings that have been relocated from rural outposts around the state in an effort to re-create life in rural villages during the 1890s. While strolling that "Loockerman Landing," you'll visit a general store, stop in a farmhouse, attend church and school, see what the blacksmith is up to, and catch up on gossip at the barbershop.

Exhibits inside the 38,000-square-foot main museum building tell the story of Delaware's largest industry, from its poultry sector to dairy and produce. You'll learn about some fascinating inventions and see old-time farm vehicles up close. Keep an eye out for a special display about the fun farmland hobby of whittling. More than 40 works by master whittler Jehu Camper are here, accompanied by a soundtrack of interviews with the artist. As of this writing, the exhibit spaces were undergoing renovation—fingers crossed that they're all spruced up by the time you arrive.

Tourism info: Kent County (Del.) Tourism

THE DOVER GREEN

Today, the Dover Green is impeccably manicured and set amid grand public buildings in a state capitol complex. But it began life in more raucous fashion. Back in the 1700s, it was the bustling center of commerce in a fledgling town, the site of fairs, open-air markets, taverns, and inns.

Visitors today can track that transition (and more) by visiting the various attractions that make up the First State Heritage Park. The little John Bell House was originally built in the mid-1700s as a workshop attached to an inn. The Old State House dates to 1791 and remained in service into the 20th century. You will find a welcome center with exhibits in the Delaware Archives. The Biggs Museum of American Art is just around the bend.

You will travel through time while moving from one site to another, meeting people whose local lives brushed up against the big sweep of history. This is where the Revolutionary soldiers marched and the U.S. Constitution was ratified. This is where a group known as the "Dover Eight" made one of the most dramatic escapes in the annals of the underground railroad. Suffragettes campaigned hard here, trying to get women the right to vote. Park staffers put extra effort into dramatizing these stories during special events held on the first Saturday of every month.

Tourism info: Kent County (Del.) Tourism

BOMBAY HOOK NATIONAL WILDLIFE REFUGE

East of Dover, Bombay Hook National Wildlife Refuge covers nearly 16,000 acres that are managed so as to be hospitable to migrating birds. But human visitors are welcome, too. A 12-mile "wildlife drive" will lead you past five short strolling trails and three elevated overlooks that offer vistas of tidal saltmarsh.

The exotic-sounding name here is not a reference to the city in India that's now called Mumbai. It's an English take on the name early Dutch settlers gave this place in the 1600s—*Boompjes Hoeck*, or "little tree point." One of those settlers, Peter Bayard, bought the *hoeck* from an Indian chief named Mechacksett for one gun, four handfuls of powder, three waistcoats, one generous supply of liquor, and one kettle.

Another cool thing to keep in mind: Bombay Hook opened as a refuge in 1937. A lot of backbreaking work went into preparation for that. The young men who built causeways and dikes, cleared undergrowth, planted 50,000 trees, put up a 90-foot observation tower, and erected the headquarters building belonged to the lone African-American-only "camp" of the Depression-era Civilian Conservation Corps. At one point, those young men were paid $30 a month, but they were required to send $25 of that back home to help their parents and siblings make it through tough times without going on the dole. The work those young men did set the foundation for an attraction that draws more than 100,000 visitors a year today.

Tourism info: Kent County (Del.) Tourism

SMYRNA ITINERARY

A gazillion cars fly past Smyrna on the Route 1 highway every year without ever pausing to get to know the place. Hey, their loss.

The town started out in the 1700s as a shipping center known as Duck Creek Cross Roads. One fun theory on how the name Smyrna arose in the early 1800s involves famed Methodist preacher Francis Asbury delivering a compelling sermon on a Biblical passage in Revelations centered on events at the "Church of Smyrna," a real-world place in present-day Turkey.

Explore the stories of the town at the Smyrna Museum, operated by the Duck Creek Historical Society and housed in two buildings that date to the 1700s. The Smyrna Opera House is a notable architectural and historical gem among the 800-and-some "contributing" buildings in the town's National Register Historic District. You might also schedule a visit to Belmont Hall, a Georgian-style mansion that dates to the 1770s.

The town has been on the upswing in recent years, so no real worries about finding good food, local libations, and worthwhile shops. If you want to get a taste of the waterfront, head east on Route 6 and find your way to the boat launch and fishing pier at Woodland Beach—that was a thriving resort at one time. There's still a sweet little stretch of beach there.

Tourism info: Kent County (Del.) Tourism

THE BAYSHORE BYWAY

Is this the prettiest drive on the Delmarva Peninsula? There are other contenders, to be sure, but you could make a pretty darn strong case for this 100-mile route running between New Castle and Lewes. The prettiest stretch to my eyes lies between Delaware City and Bowers Beach, where the Byway runs through an awe-inspiring stretch of marshland dotted with nature preserves.

Take strolls and enjoy scenic overlooks at Bombay Hook National Wildlife Refuge and the Cedar Swamp and Augustine wildlife areas, among others. Take the time to wander into the interesting old towns of Port Penn and Delaware City along the way. The Port Penn Interpretive Center is open on Saturdays in the warmer months. You can stroll the Port Penn Wetlands Trail anytime.

Tourism info: Kent County (Del.) Tourism and/or Wilmington (Del.) Tourism

DELAWARE CITY AND FORT DELAWARE

Delaware City never quite lived up to the vision of its founders, who were quite certain back in the 1800s that their brainchild of a planned town was destined to become a major metropolis. But, hey, things turned out well enough. The downtown run of shops and restaurants covers a handful of blocks, and those blocks are set opposite waterfront Battery Park. That park has the feel of an outdoor museum, thanks to well done signage telling some of the stories of the place.

In the warmer months, a ferry runs from here out to Fort Delaware, the site of a prison for captured Confederates during the Civil War. The fort is out on Pea Patch Island, which is a popular spot among birders on the prowl for herons, egrets, and ibises.

Just below town is the small Fort DuPont State Park, where you can follow a Riverview Trail alongside the Delaware and past the old gun batteries from the late 1800s and early 1900s, when the place really was a fort.

Tourism info: Wilmington (Del.) Tourism

THE CHESAPEAKE & DELAWARE CANAL

Construction of this waterway began in the 1820s, with 2,600 men—many of them Irish immigrants, many others free black laborers—earning 75 cents a day toiling with picks and shovels to cut a ditch 10 feet deep and 36 feet wide. The 14-mile ditch they dug revolutionized transportation patterns on Delmarva, as ships traveling Baltimore and Philadelphia no longer had to sail down the Chesapeake Bay and back up the oceanside.

The canal is much wider now, so much so that it accommodates humongous international cargo ships running to 700 feet long. It's the only manmade waterway in the country that dates to the 1800s and still functions as a full-fledged shipping route. You can stroll or pedal the banks of the canal by finding your way to the Michael N. Castle C&D Canal Trail. The parking areas I've used are in the vicinity of Delaware City and St. George's. Both of those towns are worth wandering.

Follow the canal across the border into Maryland to visit the C&D Canal Museum in Chesapeake City if you want to dig deeper into the stories here.

Tourism info: Wilmington (Del.) Tourism

FROM LUM'S POND TO IRON HILL

It's easy to zoom along Route 896 or Route 1 on your way to and from points north without ever stopping to explore a little. Trust me, I did it for years. Lums Pond State Park is a good place to start correcting the error of your ways. Located between Middletown on the south and Glasgow on the north, it runs to 1,800 acres and offers a number of trails wrapping around the shores of the state's largest body of freshwater. If your notion of fun includes riding zip lines and strolling the forest canopy in "Treetop Adventures," find your way to the Go Ape area of the park.

North of Glasgow and south of Interstate 95 is Iron Hill Park and Museum. A 3.2-mile loop trail here passes the remains of old mines, old homes, old bootlegging operations, and old stone walls dating to Revolutionary times. At the Iron Hill Science Center, you'll learn about fossils, insects, geology, zoology and other tidbits in an idiosyncratic collection focused on natural history. If you ask nicely, the staff there might show you the museum's previous home—it's a century-old former school that served African American students in segregation times.

Tourism info: Wilmington (Del.) Tourism

NEWARK ITINERARY

The collegiate vibe runs strong in Newark. On the campus of the University of Delaware, visit the University Gallery to see contemporary photography, printmaking, and Native American ceramics. Mechanical Hall houses the Paul R. Jones Collection of African American Art, with works by the likes of Romare Bearden, Elizabeth Catlett, and Kofi Bailey, among many others. The Mineralogical Museum in Penny Hall has interesting old rocks from various corners of the country and the world—that collection was once owned by Irenee du Pont.

In town, check to see if the Newark History Museum is open. Housed in an 1877 railroad station, it tells a slew of different stories about the people and industries that shaped this place over the centuries. The small nearby Pencader Heritage Museum is focused on the broader "Pencader Hundred" countryside, while the historic Hale Byrne House is where George Washington called a Council of War to plan for the upcoming Battle of Brandywine. Spoiler alert: That Revolutionary moment did not end in triumph for the good guys.

Stretch your legs at nearby White Clay Creek State Park. Alternatively, you could walk around campus until you find the UDairy Creamery, an entrepreneurial educational initiative the serves up first-rate sweet treats while also teaching students about dairy production, food science, and business management.

Tourism info: Wilmington (Del.) Tourism

MIDDLETOWN/ODESSA ITINERARY

Mention Middletown and what comes to mind for most folks is big box stores and new housing developments, because that's the view while passing by on the highway. But you can also wander shops and eateries along the old-time Main Street here and perhaps see what's playing at the century-old Everett Theatre.

Middletown got its name in the early 1700s because it was the halfway point on an overland trade route that linked the Bohemia River (and hence, the Chesapeake Bay) with Appoquinimink Creek (and hence, the Delaware Bay). Its first big heyday came during the late 1800s boomtimes when newfangled railroads spurred demand for peaches and other produce. Visit the Middletown Historical Society to learn about these and other stories.

Or you skip the history and go straight to spooky: At FrightLand Haunted Attractions, you can take a spooky hayride or visit one or more of four different haunted houses. If you need natural peace and quiet, find your way to the Charles E. Price Memorial Park, with its eight-acre pond.

The reason nearby Odessa is so small and quaint today goes back to those railroad boomtimes in Middletown. The line was originally supposed to run straight through Odessa (it was called Cantwell's Bridge then), but shipowners and merchants here, set in their sailing-port ways, were too suspicious of that newfangled "iron horse." They told the railroad to get lost, which is how it ended up in Middletown.

That fateful decision pays off for modern-day visitors, as you will get to stroll timeless tree-lined old streets that missed out on modern "progress." Tour the five glorious old residences that make up the Historic Homes of Odessa. The visit is pleasant all year round, but they go all out with Christmas tours.

Tourism info: Wilmington (Del.) Tourism

NEW CASTLE ITINERARY

How historic is New Castle? Way back in 1651, it was a Dutch outpost called Fort Casimir. William Penn began his American journey here, coming ashore in 1682. The town looks the historic part, too, with its charming buildings, stately trees, and red-brick streets.

Get the lay of the land at the New Castle Visitor Center on Market Street. You can watch an introductory video there and learn about the trio of properties run by the New Castle Historical Society—the Amstel House mansion (1730s), the Dutch House (late 1600s); and the hexagonal Old Library Museum (1890s). The Read House and Gardens should be on your historical hit list, too. That 1804 mansion covers 14,000 square feet and stands on a gorgeous 2.5-acre site.

At the New Castle Court House Museum you can dig a little deeper into the stories of New Castle's early days while wandering a striking old building that dates to the 1730s. Be sure to learn while there about the extraordinary events that unfolded during the 1845 escape along the Underground Railroad of the family of Sam and Emeline Hawkins.

If the weather's nice, leave plenty of time to savor the beauty of waterfront Battery Park. The cute little white building there has an interesting story to tell—it's an old ticket office from the Frenchtown New Castle Railroad, the first railway in Delaware, and an important chapter in the national story of railroading. If you're a bibliophile, make sure to include Oak Knoll Books on your hit list while wandering a town that's a joy to stroll through.

Tourism info: Wilmington (Del.) Tourism

SWEDISH WILMINGTON

A trio of sites near downtown Wilmington tell fascinating stories about the Swedish adventurers who settled in Delaware in the earliest days of European settlement. "Old Swedes" is a gorgeous stone house of worship on Church Street that dates to the late 1600s and ranks as the oldest church in the country that's still standing as originally built and still functioning for a congregation. Visitors can take a guided tour and wander an incredible old cemetery.

A few blocks away is the Fort Christina National Historic Landmark, a small park at the spot where two storied Swedish ships landed in 1637 on a mission to build a New World colony for Queen Christina. Nearby is the shipyard where a gorgeous replica of one of those ships, the *Kalmar Nyckel*, was built. Perhaps the ship will be docked there when you visit, but either way you'll be able to check out exhibits at the Copeland Maritime Museum. *Kalmar Nickel* offers regular public excursions in the warmer months, so get out under those magnificent sails if the scheduling works out.

When you're done with the Swedish angle, head to River-front Wilmington for food, libations, and more sweet scenery.

Tourism info: Wilmington (Del.) Tourism

RIVERFRONT WILMINGTON

The Cristina River may be a touristy gem today, but it used to be an industrial powerhouse. You will learn all about that while strolling a Riverwalk dotted with modern-day joys. An estimated 10,000 ships were built here between the age of schooners and World War II. Countless railroad and trolley cars came out of the bustling plants of legendary firms like Harlan & Hollingsworth; Pusey and Jones; and Jackson & Sharp.

The riverfront went into decline after World War II and became quite the civic eyesore. Eventually, however, Wilming-tonians came together and launched a big, pricey civic effort to bring it back to life. Among the attractions you'll find nowadays while strolling the Christina's banks: pretty little Tubman-Garrett Park, the Delaware Theatre Company, the Delaware Contempo-rary art museum, the Delaware Children's Museum, the Delaware Sports Museum and Hall of Fame, and the stadium of baseball's minor-league Wilmington Blue Rocks. Lots of dining, drinking, and shopping options, too.

There is a natural element as well. At Riverwalk's southern end, the DuPont Environmental Education Center rises up four stories in the midst of lush wetlands and provides commanding views of both the Wilmington skyline and the 212-acre Russell W. Peterson Urban Wildlife Refuge. An education center inside has lots of interesting exhibits. Boardwalk trails lead out over the surrounding marshlands.

Tourism info: Wilmington (Del.) Tourism

NORTH MARKET STREET WILMINGTON

For a couple of centuries in days gone by North Market Street stood at the center of civic life in Wilmington—shopping, socializing, theater, dining, and more. That changed starting in the 1960s. Rioting in the aftermath of the assassination of Rev. Martin Luther King Jr. struck one blow, and competition from newfangled malls out in the suburbs delivered another.

But Market Street is rising again, thanks to a slow-but-sure revitalization campaign over the last couple of decades. The old "Main Street" of Wilmington is buzzing once again with shops, galleries, theaters, and, especially, restaurants. Be sure to find the well-done Delaware History Museum in the 500 block and to check out the museum's Mitchell Center for African American Heritage. A couple of blocks farther up, the Grand serves up a stream of top-notch touring musicians and theatrical productions in a trio of different performance spaces—the Playhouse, the Baby Grand, and Copeland Hall.

A few blocks away in the Quaker Hill neighborhood is the

fascinating old Quaker Friends Meeting House (1815). Wander the graveyard there and find the resting place of Underground Railroad hero Thomas Garrett, who should be even more famous than he is.

Tourism info: Wilmington (Del.) Tourism

ROCKWOOD PARK AND MANSION

Located just off of Interstate 95, Wilmington's Rockwood Park covers 72 acres set around the historic Rockwood Mansion. That Rural Gothic Revival gem dates to the 1850s when Delaware-born Joseph Shipley decided to come back home and build his dream retirement house after a successful career in England as a cotton merchant. It'll be up to you whether to tour the mansion and its six-acre gardens in guided or self-guided fashion.

Along the way you'll learn about Shipley's various obsessions in life— exotic horticulture, fine art, antiques, and English gardens among them. The various parlor rooms in the mansion are filled with centuries-old English and American decorative arts. Those gardens have been meticulously restored based on old photos, plans, and receipts.

Planned in a "Gardenesque" style that blends scenes of wilderness with touches of highly cultivated beauty, the landscape at Rockwood boasts wide open lawns, sweeping vistas, and curving paths. The conservatory may be the only one of its Gothic Revival kind still standing in the United States.

More strolling awaits in nearby Bellevue State Park if you're game.

Tourism info: Wilmington (Del.) Tourism

Brandywine Park and Zoo

Take a walk on the wild side at Brandywine Park in Wilmington, which covers 178 acres and houses the small-but-fun Brandywine Zoo. Designed in the late 1800s with legendary landscape architect Frederick Law Olmsted on board as a consultant, the broader park straddles Brandywine Creek and features wooded trails, a sculpture garden, and a swinging bridge.

Two formal gardens adorn the grounds, one centered on roses and another on cherry blossoms. Five smaller gardens honor Wilmington's sister-city-style ties to communities in England, Sweden, Germany, Nigeria, and Italy.

At the zoo you'll find mammals, birds, reptiles, and amphibians from all over the world. Keep an eye out for the capybara, a South American creature with a big fat barrel of a body and a skinny little head—it ranks as the world's largest rodent.

Tourism info: Wilmington (Del.) Tourism

Nemours & Hagley

Want a taste of the glitzy side? Nemours Estate in Wilmington is a spectacular 77-room mansion built in 1909 by Alfred I. du Pont, a member of the fantastically wealthy family that founded the modern-day corporate behemoth of DuPont. The 200-plus-acre estate in the Brandywine Valley north of Wilmington features the largest formal French gardens in North America. A modestly named "Chauffeur's Garage" showcases an incredible collection of vintage luxury cars.

Nearby, at the Hagley Museum and Mansion, you can trace the explosive source of the wealth those du Ponts accumulated over the centuries. This 235-acre property includes the land where the first DuPont gunpowder mills got up and running in 1802. The first du Pont family home in America is here, too, along with old powder yards, an old machine shop, a Renaissance Revival garden, and more. Be sure to attend the frequent demonstrations of how things worked with those water wheels on the riverside and inside the machine shop. Fittingly, the museum has a special emphasis on business innovation and entrepreneurship through the centuries, including the way new businesses impact laborers and their families.

Two other nearby options to consider: Alpacas Run State Park, with its blue granite cliffs and a barn displaying folk art by Delawareans, and Rockford Park, where you can climb to the top of a century-old stone tower and take in some gorgeous views.

Tourism info: Wilmington (Del.) Tourism

WINTERTHUR MUSEUM AND GARDENS

Simultaneously a symbol of the excesses some rich folks indulge in and of their penchant for incredible generosity, Winterthur is a 175-room mansion set on 1,000 acres of preserved land. Built by the du Ponts, it served as a family home for three generations before Henry Francis du Pont decided to open it up to the public to serve as a "source of inspiration and education for all time... where visitors may enjoy as I have, not only the flowers, trees and shrubs, but also the sunlit meadows, shady wood paths, and the peace and great calm."

Displayed inside the mansion is one of the nation's finest collections of decorative arts. Nearly 90,000 items are featured, ranging from spartan Shaker furniture to over-the-top rococo masterworks. Paintings, ceramics, textiles, metalworks—it's all here.

The 60-acre garden is regarded as among the best in the nation, too. The Garden Club of America once honored Henry Francis du Pont as "one of the best, [perhaps] even the best, gardener this country has ever produced." His work grew out of a love for the local landscape, as it's set amid curving paths that honor the natural rises, twists, and turns of the Brandywine Valley. Visitors can either walk those paths or sign on for a narrated tram ride.

If you have time and energy left after the extravagances of Winterthur, the Delaware Museum of Natural History is nearby.

Tourism info: Wilmington (Del.) Tourism

LONGWOOD GARDENS

Located across the border in Kennett Square, Pennsylvania, Longwood ranks among the top landscape garden attractions in the country, with some 4,600 different types of plants and trees set on 1,000 acres of woodlands and meadows, as well as indoors in several elaborate greenhouses. The spectacular fountains are a big draw here, along with the first-rate lineup of concerts and other performing arts on the annual calendar.

Any time of year is good for visiting, but Christmas at Longwood has a special place in the hearts of countless locals—the spectacular holiday light display they put on is not to be missed. The place is thick with history, too. The Quaker farmer George Peirce who bought land here in 1700 was a natural history hobbyist who started in with planting botanical oddities. One legend says the name Longwood stems from "Long Woods," a term antislavery activists used to spread the word that this location was a stop along the Underground Railroad.

Search Longwood Gardens for info.

CHAPTER NINE:
UPPER EASTERN SHORE OF MARYLAND DESTINATIONS

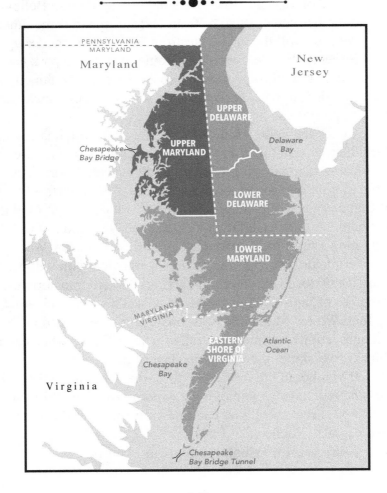

OXFORD AND ITS FERRY

When you take the Oxford-Bellevue Ferry across the Tred Avon River, you are riding the currents of centuries gone by. The first ferry here was authorized back in 1683, when the boat involved was powered by 14-foot-long sweep oars. Today's motorized crossings end on one side in Oxford and on the other in Bellevue.

Whether you cross to or from Oxford, spend some time there. You can stroll the long waterfront Strand and wander up Morris Street to dawdle over views from a waterfront park and admire a long run of gorgeous old houses. Parts of the famed Robert Morris Inn, where you can stop for a drink or a meal, date to the early 1700s.

Check the hours of the Oxford Museum, which is devoted to local history, and the Water's Edge Museum, which focuses on the African-American story of Maryland's Eastern Shore. You'll be able to browse a couple of shops as well. The waterfront Oxford Cemetery just outside of town contains the grave of (and a monument to) Tench Tilghman, who famously served as George Washington's right-hand-man during the Revolutionary War.

While driving out of or into Oxford by car you will pass the newish Oxford Conservation Park, an 86-acre transformation-in-progress of farmland into parkland as well as the fascinating little John Wesley Methodist Episcopal Church. Founded in 1838, the congregation's membership rolls for 1851 list 31 whites and 26 blacks, worshipping together in slavery times.

If you board the ferry in Oxford, that landing on the Bellevue side will have you enjoying a winding two-lane drive up to Route 33. From there, you can find your way into the touristy pleasures of St. Michaels or Easton.

Tourism info: Talbot County (Md.) Tourism

Easton Itinerary

The seat of Talbot County boasts a thriving downtown along six
or so blocks of dining and shopping in a streetscape rich in old
architecture. Be sure to see who's playing at the storied Avalon
Theatre while you're in town. On the green expanse in front of
the old courthouse is a statue that depicts Frederick Douglass in
the act of delivering a speech in the post-Civil War years in the
same town where decades earlier he had spent time in jail over a
failed attempt to escape from slavery.

Check the hours of the Talbot County Historical Society
to get the lay of the land. A walking-tour brochure available either
online or at the downtown visitor center will guide you through
the Hill, one of the nation's most historic African-American communities—free blacks first moved in here clear back in the 1780s.
Along the way you'll find a mural honoring Talbot native son
Frederick Douglass.

For a moment of serenity, drive a little ways down Washington Street, passing the hospital and keeping eyes peeled for
a little sign that marks the long driveway leading back to the
Quaker Third Haven Meeting House (405 S. Washington St.).
The oldest of the buildings on the grounds there dates to 1681 and
probably ranks as the oldest surviving Quaker meeting house in
the country. In the early days, the faithful would arrive on boats
along the river that then ran deep and wide in back of the property.

In the countryside north of town, the Pickering Creek
Audubon Center has more than four miles of walking trails along-
side that creek and through forestlands and wetlands. In town,
Idyllwild Park offers a pleasant and relaxing bit of greenery.

Tourism info: Talbot County (Md.) Tourism

ST. MICHAELS ITINERARY

St. Michaels may be known far and wide today as a tourist destination, but its roots are as hardscrabble as any town on Maryland's Eastern Shore. Dig into the town's rough-and-tumble times at the St. Michaels Museum at St. Mary's Square. There will be materials there as well on the great freedom fighter Frederick Douglass, who lived here in a key stretch of his adolescence.

Get the broader sweep of things at the Chesapeake Bay Maritime Museum. With multiple exhibit buildings on 18 waterfront acres, plus a "floating fleet" of nearly 100 vessels, it's one of the top facilities of its kind in the whole country.

A leisurely stroll through one of Delmarva's prettiest downtowns offers diversions aplenty, from high-end dining and shopping to quaint ice cream shops and locally made libations. Find the pretty little St. Michaels Nature Trail for a stroll. You can get out on the water by signing up in advance for cruises on a big boat (Patriot Cruises) or a small one (the skipjack *H.M. Krentz*). On the way there or back, take the winding back roads to the Oxford-Bellevue Ferry and drive aboard for the trip across the pretty Tred Avon River.

Tourism info: Talbot County (Md.) Tourism

TILGHMAN ISLAND

The centuries-old watermen's community of Tilghman Island lies a dozen or so miles beyond St. Michaels along Route 33. Crossing the drawbridge there, you'll find a sweet old general store, postcard-pretty Dogwood Harbor, and several interesting restaurants. The best place to get in touch with the stories of the island is the Tilghman Watermen's Museum, another of Delmarva's wonderful little museums.

Take note of the museum's exterior, which is designed in an odd shape that mimics the letter W. Local lore has islanders back in the 1890s believing that this design delivered better airflow on hot summer days. As far as anyone has been able to tell so far, the design is unique to Tilghman and nearby Sherwood. Seven W houses are still standing, but only this and one other are in near-original condition. Inside the museum, you'll learn about the famous Tilghman Packing Company, the history of boat builders, the lives of watermen, big storms, and more. In recent years, the museum has been open on weekends April through November or by appointment.

If you are in a mood for cruising pretty backroads on the way there or back, keep an eye out for Bozman-Neavitt Road, which heads through the two small towns of that name, and Claiborne Road, which leads up into the town of that name and ends in a view of a famous old steamboat wharf and the broad Eastern Bay.

Tourism info: Talbot County (Md.) Tourism

THE FREDERICK DOUGLASS DRIVING TOUR

A fascinating all-American story unfolds along this Talbot County itinerary. How did a baby boy born into slavery in a one-room cabin in 1818 manage to become one of the most important men of his time?

Broken into four sections, the tour explores Douglass's birth and early childhood in that cabin, then moves through the times of struggle and oppression he endured in youth and adolescence. You'll learn, too, about his eventual escape from slavery and subsequent rise to fame as an orator, writer, and antislavery activist. The itinerary here stretches into the years after the Civil War, too. Douglass made several visits back to his home turf in his later years, including one where he paid a visit to his former owner as that man lay on his deathbed.

The tour will have you wandering a mix of two-lane backroads and interesting towns. FYI for the future, Talbot County is in the process of building what promises to be a first-rate Frederick Douglass Park on Tuckahoe Creek. The site of that park is on the driving-tour itinerary—consider it a glimpse of things to come.

Tourism info: Talbot County (Md.) Tourism

UPPER HARRIET TUBMAN UNDERGROUND RAILROAD BYWAY

While born and raised down in Dorchester County, Md., Harriet Tubman was living up in Caroline County when she made the fateful decision in 1849 to make a run from slavery and seek freedom in the north. Her parents had deep connections on this rural landscape and almost certainly operated an Underground Railroad "station" from their home near the little town of Choptank.

This stretch of the Tubman Byway is a driving tour that runs from stop to stop in lily-pad fashion at sites that touch not just on Tubman's journey, but on those of other, lesser-known champions of freedom as well. You'll meet the Rev. Samuel Green, a "conductor" who did prison time for the crime of owning a copy of the book *Uncle Tom's Cabin*. You'll learn about the meticulous, brilliant planning that Moses Viney put into his journey out of bondage. The roots of Underground Railroad conductor and chronicler William Still are here, too. If you want to get a feel for the way "free" blacks lived in slavery times, be sure to find the Webb Cabin and the William Still Interpretive Center.

Tourism info: Harriet Tubman Underground Railroad Byway and/or Caroline County (Md.) Tourism

WYE ISLAND

One of the joys of visiting Wye Island is the ride out there. Once off the Route 50 highway, it will lead you through a run of farmland where scientists have been working for decades to develop new techniques and strategies for finding the right mix between productivity and environmental sustainability. This Maryland Agricultural Experiment Station is perhaps most famous for its research into the thriving (and photogenic) herd of Black Angus cattle you will see along Carmichael and Wye Island roads.

That latter road ends in the 3,000-acre Wye Island Natural Resource Management Area. The place is managed to be welcoming to wildlife, but you're welcome, too. Five hiking trails lead out to or run alongside various pretty waterways—the Wye River, Granary Creek, Bigwood Cove, and Dividing Creek among them.

Much of the land here was once owned by William Paca, a signer of the Declaration of Independence. The forests here now were all farmland back then, with vast swaths of tobacco or wheat swaying in the fields. There were some orchards, too, along with a windmill, a vineyard, and a brewery. The closest modern-day example of the latter is just down the road—it's called Ten Eyck Brewing Company.

Tourism info: Queen Anne's County (Md.) Tourism and/or Talbot County (Md.) Tourism

WYE MILLS

The tiny, picturesque village of Wye Mills is as good a place as any on the Delmarva Peninsula to get a glimpse back at colonial times. Old Wye Mill first started running back in the late 1600s. The operation helped feed George Washington's troops during their frozen, hungry winter at Valley Forge. Now primarily a tourist attraction, the mill gets up and running a couple of Saturdays every month. Nearby is Wye Oak State Park, which showcased a famously ancient oak before that tree toppled over during a storm in 2002. A genetic clone is now growing in its stead. Even without the old tree, it's still a sweet spot for a picnic.

Just up the street is one of Maryland's oldest churches— Old Wye Episcopal, where the building dates to the 1720s and the grounds boast a gorgeous old graveyard. The story of that parish tracks the history of its denomination. Built as an Anglican church tied closely with the English government, Old Wye drew such big crowds in colonial times that half the worshippers had to stand and everyone complained about how "small" and "incommodious" the church was.

Then came the Revolution. For obvious reasons, everything tied to the bad-guy Brits fell into disrepute. The local economy went into a tailspin after the war. By 1820, Old Wye had just 14 members. By the 1830s, it was closed. The building was used as a cattle stable for a while, then returned again to the role of struggling country church. Finally, in the 1940s, it found a guardian angel in the person of Arthur Houghton Jr., a richer-than-god businessman who devoted a big chunk of his fortune to various historic renovation efforts, including this one.

Tourism info: Talbot County (Md.) Tourism and/or Queen Anne's County (Md.) Tourism

DENTON ITINERARY

Set along the upper Choptank River, Denton is a quiet, pretty town with lots of stories to tell. Get started digging into those tales at the Rural Life Museum and the Wharves of Choptank Visitor Center. The downtown has a modest collection of stores and restaurants. Find your way to the "Artsway" stretch of Fourth Street to visit a fiber arts center and the county arts council. The grand county courthouse (1895) stands on a rise that used to be called "Pig Point." President Franklin Delano Roosevelt visited in 1938 to give a Labor Day address that was broadcast nationally by radio.

Just outside of downtown, across the river, stands the old Tuckahoe Neck Meeting House. The interior is open only rarely, but the strikingly spare 1803 building speaks even from the outside to the long, rich, and important history of Quaker activism in this area. Below town is little Martinak State Park, where you can admire the Choptank and explore skinny little Watts Creek. Some historians believe that a Choptank Indian settlement was located here in Native American times.

Tourism info: Caroline County (Md.) Tourism

ADKINS ARBORETUM AND TUCKAHOE STATE PARK

Back in the early 1960s, state officials wanted to build a sprawling manmade lake near Ridgely in Caroline County as a tourist attraction akin to Western Maryland's Deep Creek Lake. But after buying up a bunch of land, they learned by way of a geological survey that such a lake might not be able to hold its water. What we ended up with instead is a fabulous consolation prize: Tuckahoe State Park covers 4,000 acres of woodlands and streams with 25 miles of hiking trails. Fishing and paddling are popular, too—not just along Tuckahoe Creek, but also on the smaller lake that the state eventually did build, which clocks in at 60 acres. Both valley and creek take their name from the Indian word for arrow arum, a plant that produces an edible, potato-like root that helped sustain Native American tribes.

At the nearby 400-acre Adkins Arboretum, you will find five more miles of hiking trails leading through woodlands and alongside meadows. The most popular trail is probably Blockston Branch, while my favorite is the short-but-sweet River Birch Allee. Be sure to visit the goats who help out by chomping up invasive plant species—they are great fun to gawk at. The arboretum boasts 600 species of native plants and trees. The visitor center often has interesting nature-themed art shows. A couple of times a year, the Arboretum brings in artists who create temporary works that appear in the great outdoors, right amid the trees and streams.

Tourism info: Caroline County (Md.) Tourism

TWO FARMING HEARTLAND ITINERARIES

The scenes you will see along the two-lane roads that run through the farming heartland of the Upper Eastern Shore are classic Americana. Sun-drenched fields of corn and soybeans, interspersed with evocative old farmhouses, barns, and churches. One possibility for a five-town road-tripping itinerary would start in Ridgely, which had its heyday during the strawberry boom of the late 1800s and early 1900s. The restored train station there is where bevies of berries were loaded up for trips to big-city markets. You can walk a little rail trail while there. Just to the north is

Greensboro, where you can admire lots of pretty old homes and stop in the itty-bitty Benjamin House Visitor Center. Maybe make an appointment to see the Greensboro Museum, too—it's the work of dedicated local history buffs.

Make the run through quaint Goldsboro before turning west toward Sudlersville. If the timing's right, you can get the lay of the land at the interesting Sudlersville Train Station Museum. Be sure to stop and pose for a photo with the statue of native son Jimmie Foxx, a baseball hall of famer. Godrey Farms is the place to stop for produce. Have a beer at Patriot Acres Farm Brewery. Make your way up to Millington from there. Nearby is the new Cypress Branch State Park, a 314-acre expanse for hiking, picnicking, and fishing in a little pond.

If you are on the lower end of the Upper Eastern Shore, here's an alternative itinerary. Head east out of Easton on Dover Road, crossing the Choptank River into blink-and-you'll-miss-it Bethlehem. The post office here is a longstanding December destination for local folks who want that postmark on their Christmas cards. In Preston, you can visit the Preston Historical Society and wander the grounds of the old Linchester Mill. Continue on into Federalsburg, home of the well done Federalsburg Historical Society.

Tourism info: Caroline County (Md.) Tourism, Queen Anne's County (Md.) Tourism, Kent County (Md.) Tourism, and/or Talbot County (Md.) Tourism

KENT ISLAND ITINERARY

The folks who never get off the Route 50 concrete jungle on the Eastern Shore side of the Chesapeake Bay Bridge end up regarding Kent Island as a sea of little shopping centers and fast-food joints. In fact, the place offers one sweet detour after another. The quaint little hideaway of Stevensville has an itty bitty downtown where you can shop for antiques, grab a snack, and wander past buildings that seem to rise straight out of days gone by. Take the pretty ride a few miles south to Romancoke, stopping at little Matapeake State Park and then keeping on to a dead-end at in a gorgeous 650-foot-long fishing pier that serves up fabulous Chesapeake views.

Farther along, in Chester, stop in the Chesapeake Heritage & Visitors Center to see exhibits and gather up local travel into. While there, to take the shore stroll out to Ferry Point Park to enjoy the sweet views. You'll find waterfront fun in abundance at Kent Narrows, which is dotted with marinas, crab houses, and tiki-style bars. Just up the road in Grasonville is the Chesapeake Bay Environmental Center, where you can wander trails and rent kayaks to explore 300-plus acres of pristine nature.

If you time your Kent Island visit to fall on the first Saturday of the month, that's when a network of little historic sites operating under the umbrella of the Kent Island Heritage Society usually open their doors. One favorite of mine is the Kirwan House, featuring an old general store filled with fascinating throwback merchandise, much of it straight from the collection of the family that used to run the place.

Tourism info: Queen Anne's County (Md.) Tourism

THOSE KENT ISLAND TRAILS

The slower way to explore Kent Island is on two feet or two wheels, as a pair of scenic trails rank among the island's most popular attractions. You will find the westernmost end of the Cross Island Trail tucked in the back of an industrial park near

Stevensville. That trail runs 6.5 miles (and will soon be expanded) through farms, forests, and meadows. You'll cross over several creeks on wooden bridges on the way to the Chesapeake Heritage & Visitor Center. From that point you can easily find your way to the dining and drinking joys of Kent Narrows.

The South Island Trail runs for seven miles from little Matapeake State Park, where you can stroll a sweet little beach, down to the Romancoke and its glorious fishing pier. One thing to think about along the way: Kent Island was the first place Europeans set up shop in Maryland, thanks to an early adventurer named William Claiborne. He bought Kent Island from the native Susquehannocks for a collections of tools, trinkets, and cloth. No one knows exactly where he and his men built their first fort, but it was down there somewhere on the way to Romancoke.

Tourism info: Queen Anne's County (Md.) Tourism

CHESTERTOWN ITINERARY

Chestertown ranks as the most colonial place on Maryland's Eastern Shore. Founded in 1706, it was designated early on as one of just six Royal Ports of Entry in Maryland and soon grew into the colony's second largest city, after Annapolis. Today, it ranks second in the state to Annapolis in a related category—the number of still-standing buildings that date to before the American Revolution. Your first order of business here is strolling along a gorgeous waterfront and then up toward downtown while gawking at those old buildings. Wander over to Wilmer Park while you're at it.

The downtown is full of fun diversions—bakeries, coffee shops, boutiques, and galleries. Spend some time in the Bordley History Center, home of the Kent County Historical Society. The town is rich in African American heritage as well. The Charles

Sumner Post began life as a meeting hall for local veterans who served with the Colored Troops during the Civil War—it's probably the only building of its kind left standing in Maryland, and one of only two left in the whole country. Today, it's a combination exhibit hall and performance space.

The schooner *Sultana* needs to be on your must-see list as well. The work of master boat builder John Swain and a small army of volunteers, it is a meticulous re-creation of a 1768 British revenue cutter that now serves primarily as a floating classroom for school kids and teachers, but there are regular open-to-the-public sails as well. Chestertown is big with artists, too—a nice starting point on that aspect of this journey is at the cooperative gallery run by the nonprofit RiverArts.

Tourism info: Kent County (Md.) Tourism

THE CHESTERTOWN COUNTRYSIDE

The Kent County countryside west of Chestertown serves up lots of sweet little vistas. Start by visiting the churchyard at St. Paul's Episcopal, 7579 Sandy Bottom Rd. The little vestry house here was built before the Revolution, in 1766. The earliest sections of the main church building go back even further, to 1713. The churchyard covers 19 gorgeous shady acres set beside a pond and highlighted by one of the Eastern Shore's most beautiful cemeteries. Ironically, this serenely contemplative spot is the final resting place of the famously raucous and irreverent Hollywood actress Tallulah Bankhead.

Along nearby Ricaud's Branch Road you can find your way to the Chesapeake Farms, an agricultural, environmental, and wildlife research facility operated by a DuPont spinoff called

Corteva Agriscience. The map to a 14-stop, self-guided auto tour of the 3,000-acre property showing off the various projects under way here is available both online and at the farm office.

If you are a War of 1812 buff, you will want to visit Caulk's Field on Tolchester Beach Road—a small but fascinating battle unfolded there in 1814 while the Brits were getting ready to mount their ill-fated attack on Baltimore.

Tourism info: Kent County (Md.) Tourism

MASSEY AIR MUSEUM

The romantic "aerodromes" from the early days of flight have been disappearing slowly but surely since their 1930s heyday. That's the sad development that led a handful of old-school aviation aficionados to re-create those aerodrome glory days in the upper reaches of Kent County, Md. Basically, they planted a 3,000-foot-long runway in a cornfield and then set about building from there.

Find your way to the Massey Aerodrome along Route 313, on the other side of the Route 301 highway at Galena. The Aerodrome also houses the Massey Air Museum, where you can chat with knowledgeable volunteers, observe restoration projects, check out classic flying machines, and peruse a library of old magazines and books. It's the kind of place that give these instructions to visitors: "Pick up a tour guide sheet in the lobby. Feel free to ask questions. If you don't see us, we may be working in the shop or outside." The closest bits of food and shopping will be up the road in Galena or down the road in Millington.

Tourism info: Kent County (Md.) Tourism

ROCK HALL AND EASTERN NECK

The Chesapeake Bay served as a transportation superhighway during Revolutionary times, and the town of Rock Hall ranked back then as a busy rest stop. George Washington, Thomas Jefferson, and lots of other historical bigwigs made pit stops here while shuttling between Virginia and the then-capital city of Philadelphia.

Nowadays, the town lies off the beaten path, by way of a scenic drive from Chestertown along Route 20. The place takes pride in its old-school fishing-village vibe. The downtown has an interesting little mix of shops and restaurants, while the waterfront marinas offer dining, drinking, and boat rentals. You can visit a little Waterman's Museum by stopping the store at Haven Harbour Marina and signing out a key.

Follow Route 445 out of town to explore the nearby Eastern Neck National Wildlife Refuge, which covers a 2,000-plus acre island that offers hiking paths, kayaking trails, and wildlife overlooks. Be sure to visit the Wickes Historic Site at the refuge—that's named for a family that owned the island for the 252 years between 1650 and 1902.

The most famous of the Wickes was Lambert, a merchant-ship captain who retrofitted his commercial vessels for war and became quite the hero during the Revolutionary War. Here is an obscure bit of trivia about Wickes: It's in his honor that the two iron balls that are placed on either side of a ship's compass—they help "iron" out the natural magnetic variations that pop up while traveling—came to be called "Lamberts" in the maritime world.

Tourism info: Kent County (Md.) Tourism

TURNER'S CREEK

The Kent County backroads make for pleasant wandering at almost every turn. A little way east of Betterton is postcard-pretty Turner's Creek Landing, named for that tributary of the nearby Sassafras River. Spend some time in the 147-acre Turner's Creek Park and the 1,200-acre Sassafras Natural Resources Management Area. You can hike there along nine miles of trails through woods and meadows, enjoying some fabulous views of the water along the way.

Also at Sassafras you can stop in the Knock's Folly Visitor Center, though it might require making an advance appointment. Parts of that house date to the 1700s. Exhibits inside tell the story of a local Indian tribe, the Tockwogh, as well as about Captain John Smith's visit with them. Natural history is on the agenda here as well.

Near Turner's Creek Landing is the Kent Museum, where you can admire lots of antique farm equipment. The interior of the museum is only open a couple of times a month, so check on the hours if you have your heart set on getting in. You can wander the grounds anytime, however, passing an old country graveyard that dates to Revolutionary times and several sweet old buildings still standing as remnants of the past.

Tourism info: Kent County (Md.) Tourism

BETTERTON BEACH AND ITS BACKROADS

Upper Kent County is quiet nowadays, but that wasn't always the case. A pair of big-league tourist attractions drew big-city folks here in droves during the heyday of steamboats to enjoy beaches, carnival rides, dining, dancing, movies, and myriad other pleasures served up by resorts at Tolchester and Betterton Beach.

You can drive today out to the site of old Tolchester, but there is nothing really to see or explore. Betterton Beach, on the other hand, still delivers glimpses of its glorious days. On a five-acre waterfront park, you can stroll a short boardwalk, frolic on a sandy beach, and climb up a little bluff for sweet Sassafras River views. There's a bathhouse for changing and a fishing pier for anglers. The jellyfish don't cause near as much trouble for swimmers up here as they do in the lower Bay.

Be sure to make your way back up into town. Some old boarding-house-style hotels still stand amid more modern condos. The Betterton Beach Heritage Museum, located in the town's community center, will put you in touch with lots of stories from those old glory days.

Tourism info: Kent County (Md.) Tourism

THE HERMAN HIGHWAY

In spending time along the Augustine Herman Highway, perhaps you will be able soak up some inspiration from that Bohemian immigrant. Born in 1605, Herman had a gift in life for seeing the way toward a prosperous future. The road named in his honor runs in a north-south line through his old stomping grounds on the Upper Eastern Shore.

266

He is most famous as a cartographer—he created the most accurate map of the Chesapeake Bay at a time when such a map was as valuable a tool in navigating life and business as the internet is today. Herman planted grapes on his Bohemia Manor Farm—he was likely the first person to make wine on Delmarva. Five centuries later, the wine industry is thriving. His map-making work led him to propose the building of a canal—it took 150 or so years for the world to come around and see things his way. The Chesapeake & Delaware Canal, still up and running today, opened in the 1820s.

After crossing that canal southbound, you will make your way through several little towns. This route is not filled with the fancy restaurants and museums of more touristy locales, but you will find a smattering of food, drink, and shopping. First up on that southbound trail is one of Maryland's newest state parks, named for the Bohemia River on which it sits. The 460-acre site offers hiking trails and wildlife viewing as of this writing, with a fuller build-out planned for years to come. Two wineries (Chateau BuDe and Broken Spoke) are about the work of keeping that five-century-old Herman innovation alive.

The small town of Cecilton has links to Herman, too. He tried but failed to start up a town in honor of his friend Cecilius Calvert, but it eventually got done—Cecilton was founded in 1864. Next up is the Sassafras River, with another little burg, Georgetown. Look up the history of the Kitty Knight House there if you are interested in War of 1812 stories. Herman's highway then runs into interesting little Galena before turning to the southwest, running past yet another winery (Crow Vineyard), then through Kennedyville and on toward Chestertown.

Tourism info: Cecil County (Md.) Tourism and/or Kent County (Md.) Tourism

CHESAPEAKE CITY AND THE C&D CANAL

With its sweet waterfront and interesting shops and restaurants, downtown Chesapeake City might look at first like just another small-town gem on the Delmarva Peninsula. But you can start to sense its uniqueness by way of the bridge that towers over this downtown. With a steep, horseshoe-like shape, it reaches up 140 feet so as to accommodate the thousands of cargo ships that pass under it along the Chesapeake & Delaware Canal every year.

Chesapeake City took shape in the earliest days of that waterway. When the canal opened on Oct. 17, 1829, just two buildings stood here. Within a decade, it had grown into a town of 300.

The population is a smidge under 700 now. In addition to wandering the downtown, you'll want to check out the C&D Canal Museum to learn about how the canal revolutionized transportation patterns on the Eastern Shore in the 1800s. Be sure to take a look at the old water wheel and the incredible small-scale model of the old James Adams Floating Theatre that used to put on shows along this canal and on rivers all over the Chesapeake. After that, find your way to the Ben Cardin Trail and stroll or pedal your way along the banks of this historic waterway. The trailhead is on the north bank at the end of Lock Street, so you'll need to cross that big swooping bridge to get there.

The canal ends its run across the state line in Delaware City, another town well worth visiting.

Tourism info: Cecil County (Md.) Tourism

MOUNT HARMON PLANTATION

The story of this old tobacco plantation dates to the 1650s, a period when old maps referred to the peninsula where the plantation stands as "World's End." The name fits even today, as Mount Harmon is indeed out in the middle of nowhere, set along pretty creeks near the Sassafras River in Cecil County. While wandering its 200 acres, you'll be able to tour the 1730 manor house, visit the colonial kitchen, admire the serpentine-walled boxwood garden, see the slave quarters, walk nature trails, check out the tobacco "prize house," and see exhibits in the Carriage House Education & Discovery Center.

The story of how this modern-day experience came into being is fascinating, too. The property stayed in the Harmon family all the way up to 1927, but then landed in the hands of other owners. In a labor of love for her family's heritage, the Harmon descendant Marguerite du Pont de Villiers Boden bought the property back in the 1960s, then brought in a first-rate team to restore it to its former glory. Open May through September, Mount Harmon's "World's End" location is 10 or so miles south east of Cecilton.

Tourism info: Cecil County (Md.) Tourism

ELK NECK STATE PARK

The drive from the town of North East is a glorious affair, winding up and down hills along Old Elk Neck Road and then Turkey Point Road, which ends at the lowermost point in Elk Neck State Park. From the parking area there, an easy three-quarters-of-a-mile stroll leads out a tall bluff where Turkey Point Light has been standing since 1833, alerting mariners that it's time for them to turn if they want to go up the Elk River and into the Chesa-peake & Delaware Canal.

Wrapped in white stucco and topped by a black roof and a glass light chamber, the lighthouse is open for a few hours on Saturdays and Sundays in the warmer months, which is when visitors have the opportunity to climb the 31 steps inside and visit a little gift shack outside. But the trail is open every day, and the stunning scenery out on this bluff is worth the walk whether the beacon interior is open or not. Just 35 feet tall, Turkey Point is perched atop a 100-foot-high bluff. Measuring from the water, it ranks as the third tallest of the 82 beacons that have done duty around the Chesapeake Bay over the centuries.

Turkey Point Light has a second claim to fame. During 19th- and 20th-century periods when men dominated the lighthouse-keeper game, Turkey Point had four different female keepers. Women were in charge for 89 of the 115 years when the facility was, um, manned on a 24/7 basis.

Leave plenty of time to explore the larger state park, which covers 2,500 acres and offers 12 miles of hiking trails as well as the usual array of park facilities.

Tourism info: Cecil County (Md.) Tourism

NORTH EAST AND CHARLESTOWN

The first Europeans to settle on the banks of the North East River did so because the inland streams flow a little faster through this hilly terrain. The town that bears the river's name sprung up around early gristmills and ironworks powered by the force of that moving water.

That water remains the main attraction here today, but now with a focus on recreation, as the town is quite popular with boaters, anglers, and hunters. Visit North East Community Park on the riverfront to take in the scenery and see the old decoys and vintage marine gear on display at the Upper Bay Museum. Main Street in North East is a short-but-sweet collection of shops and restaurants, with antiques and comfort foods at the top of the agenda. Just beyond that business district is pretty St. Mary Anne's Episcopal Church, which dates to the mid-1700s.

From North East, take a short ride along Old Philadelphia Road into the little waterfront town of Charlestown. Its founders were supremely confident back in 1742 that the new settlement would soon outpace then-13-year-old Baltimore and become the biggest metropolis on the upper bay. Nothing remotely metropolitan ever developed, of course, but you'll enjoy sweet views of the North East River and more than two dozen National Register buildings from the 1700s and 1800s that once served as homes, taverns, and inns.

Tourism info: Cecil County (Md.) Tourism

ELKTON ITINERARY

The northernmost destination here on the Upper Eastern Shore ranks nowadays as a distant suburb of Baltimore on the south and Wilmington on the north, so you might run into annoying traffic along Route 40 or Interstate 95. But the role of crossroads community is nothing new in Elton, which back in colonial times served a way station on a different kind of highway. Revolutionary-War-era VIPs traveling from Norfolk, Annapolis, and other western shore locales often made their way to Philadelphia by sailing across the bay and up the Elk River, then traveling overland from Elkton to the Delaware River.

The town stands on property seized from a rich guy

named Robert Alexander as punishment for the way he got a little too friendly with a British general during that Revolutionary War. The historic downtown has a touch of Western Maryland about it, with a winding, slightly hilly Main Street serving up views of distant church steeples. A decent number of shops, restaurants, and galleries lie along a three-or-so block stretch. The Cecil County Historical Society always seems to have interesting stuff on display. Throughout much of the 1800s, Elkton continued to play its role as a crossroads town. One of the first steamboats to serve on the Chesapeake Bay, The Eagle, ran between Baltimore and Elkton. The railroad arrived in 1831.

An Elkton oddity: For a stretch of 25 years during the early 1900s, the town ranked as the quickie-wedding capital of the East Coast, its Main Street lined with more than 20 wedding chapels. Lots of famous people got married in Elkton—actors Cornel Wilde, Joan Fontaine, Martha Raye, and Debbie Reynolds among them.

Tourism info: Cecil County (Md.) Tourism

ABOUT SECRETS OF THE EASTERN SHORE

Thank you so much for spending time with this book! The husband-and-wife duo of writer Jim Duffy and photographer Jill Jasuta created Secrets of the Eastern Shore to celebrate and share the joys of the Delmarva Peninsula in words, pictures, and products. The pair has lived near the Choptank River in Cambridge, Md. since 2004.

Duffy started out in newspaper journalism in his hometown of Chicago, then moved into magazine writing and book projects after moving east. Jasuta started as a newspaper writer, too, before transitioning into graphic design and photography. Both have won numerous awards for their work over the years.

Visit their website at SecretsoftheEasternShore.com to see what the pair have been up to lately. That site has an ever-changing array of interesting tales, sweet photos, and travel tips, along with the full line of Secrets of the Eastern Shore books, photo prints, Delmarva-themed greeting cards, and other products.

Month of Fundays!
You should subscribe to the Month of Fundays newsletter. It connects you with up-to-the-minute info on upcoming events all over the Delmarva Peninsula, including both the ones in this book and many others.

Sign up on the website: SecretsoftheEasternShore.com. Or send an email and I'll sign you up manually: SecretsoftheEasternShore@gmail.com.

Delmarva Stories, Trips, Photographs, & More:
SecretsoftheEasternShore.com
Facebook.com/SecretsoftheEasternShore

Other Secrets of the Eastern Shore Books:
Eastern Shore Road Trips #1:
27 One-Day Adventures on Delmarva

Tubman Travels:
32 Underground Railroad Journeys on Delmarva

Eastern Shore Road Trips #2:
26 MORE One-Day Adventures on Delmarva

You Wouldn't Believe:
44 Strange and Wondrous Delmarva Tales

Bookstores, retail shops, and other purchase options:
SecretsoftheEasternShore.com/product-category/books

Feedback:
SecretsoftheEasternShore@gmail.com; 443.477.4490

ABOUT THE TEAM

Jim Duffy wrote most of the book. A co-founder of Secrets of the Eastern Shore, he has written five books (so far!) on travel, culture, and heritage in the Delmarva Peninsula. See what Duffy has been up to lately: SecretsoftheEasternShore.com

Jill Jasuta designed the cover. A co-founder of Secrets of the Eastern Shore, she is a photographer, graphic designer, and writer. Check out her latest work here:
Facebook.com/JillJasutaPhotography
Instagram.com/JillJasutaPhotography
SecretsoftheEasternShore.com/product-category/print

Paul Clipper wrote quite a few of the event summaries and designed the interior pages of the book. An award-winning newspaper writer and magazine publisher, he has written several books about the art, adventure, and history of dirt-bike riding. He is also an amateur luthier and makes guitars out of cigar boxes for fun. Search his author name at Amazon books for more.

Makena Duffy wrote a good number of the event summaries. She is a photographer, cinematographer, artist, and talented wordsmith who lives in the New York City area.

We all thank you for spending a little time with our work. Here's hoping that our efforts help you find a little extra joy in your Delmarva wanderings.

Shore Bets!